THE
MOONSHOT
GAME

RAHUL CHANDRA

THE
MOONSHOT
GAME

ADVENTURES OF AN INDIAN
VENTURE CAPITALIST

PORTFOLIO
PENGUIN

An imprint of Penguin Random House

PORTFOLIO

USA | Canada | UK | Ireland | Australia
New Zealand | India | South Africa | China

Portfolio is part of the Penguin Random House group of companies
whose addresses can be found at global.penguinrandomhouse.com

Published by Penguin Random House India Pvt. Ltd
7th Floor, Infinity Tower C, DLF Cyber City,
Gurgaon 122 002, Haryana, India

First published in Portfolio by Penguin Random House India 2019

10 9 8 7 6 5 4 3 2 1

ISBN 9780670091201

For sale in the Indian Subcontinent only

Typeset in Adobe Garamond Pro by Manipal Digital Systems, Manipal
Printed at Replika Press Pvt. Ltd, India

www.penguin.co.in

To
the founders who have been, the founders who are,
and the founders who will be

Contents

Contents

Acknowledgements

This book, the story of a venture capitalist investing in India over the last decade, is my earnest effort to capture the emotions, upheavals and learnings compounding the seemingly clinical world of venture investments.

My editor, Lohit, has been instrumental in making me think about writing about my experiences in the first place, so all those who regret buying this book can blame him. He has been immensely patient while gently nudging me to complete the manuscript through a period full of intense activity for me.

I consider myself fortunate to have operated as a VC since the early days. My work owes itself to the power of entrepreneurship. The power that has demonstrated over and over again that it is possible to take a thought and create a valuable business out of it.

I would not be on this journey if I didn't have the support of three mentors early in my life.

Amarjeet Singh, my boss at my first job at SEBI, taught me the value of honest work. His single-minded dedication to his job was the gold standard that a young management trainee was exposed to.

At Quantum Financial, Ajit Dayal taught me to think on my own. Travelling in his car after a meeting, I was initially stumped but eventually well-prepared for his question, 'So what do you think?' For a twenty-five-year-old, learning to have a mental construct that supports naive opinions was an invaluable training. Ajit's lifelong quest for the 'honest truth' has inspired several generations of 'truth seekers' like me.

My entry in the VC world started fortuitously. Somshankar Das, a VC from Silicon Valley, hired me as the first employee at Walden International's India-focused fund. I learnt my first lessons from Som, who was a general partner at Walden's Palo Alto office, tasked with the additional responsibility of running the India fund. Som allayed my fears about joining a line of work I had very little idea of. Som's belief in me has carried on for over two decades and his pushing me into venture capital helped me set the course of my life.

A VC's journey owes itself to founders. Founders are the teachers who help VCs get better at their job and determine their success. I would like to thank all the founders I have worked with in the last twenty years: Ronnie Screwvala, Vinay Chajjlani, Rajesh Reddy, Dhruv and Piyush Khaitan, Anjan Lahiri, Raju Reddy, Arjun Malhotra, Neeraj Gokhale, Tom Lerone, Dan Reed, Deep Kalra, Phani Pandrangi, Padmaja Reddy, P.N. Vasudevan, the late Ajay Oak, Sanjay Chaturvedi,

Vishal Gupta, Abhijit Bose, Raviteja Dodda, Zishaan Hayath, Siddharth Gupta, Manish Rathi, Kapil Raizada, Arjun Zachariah and Sameer Grover.

I owe a lot of my early learnings to the lessons I learnt while investing in Silicon Valley—my colleagues at Walden who took me under their wings and taught me the ropes of the business: Lip Bu Tan, Danial Faizullabhoy, Rakinder Grover, Brian Chiang and Mary Coleman.

My co-founders at Helion, whose trust and confidence I am grateful for, were my co-pilots through many of the learnings that are captured in this book. Thanks to Ashish Gupta for being the ideal mentor who helped me grow as a person while becoming a better investor; Sanjeev, who taught me to be dispassionate about evaluating founders and to think long-term, especially when things are tough; Kanwal's infectious enthusiasm and optimism kept me going through many dark nights of disappointment.

And above all, I am grateful for the support of my family. My parents encouraged me to be independent-minded about life's major decisions and helped me to overcome disappointments with their selfless love. Their belief set the bedrock for me to own the outcomes of my decisions. They somehow managed to raise an eternally optimistic child who could deal with delayed gratification before the term was coined. I feel these two traits have played the most significant parts in my journey as a VC.

My wife, Vandana, has been the rock on which many lives come to anchor. She has withstood long periods of solo parenting, tough times and uncertainty. Without the sacrifices she has made and the encouragement she provides, this journey would not have been possible. I hope my children, Nandini and Varun, read this book someday and understand what kept a mobile phone glued to their father's ears through their growing-up years.

1

A country with a growing middle class, millions of engineers and thousands of back offices building products for global customers. A new venture capitalist (VC) fund that would work collaboratively with entrepreneurs. Past success in building start-ups. This was our sales pitch to whoever cared to listen in the summer of 2005.

The four co-founders of Helion—Sanjeev Agarwal, Ashish Gupta, Kanwaljit Singh and I—were traversing North America, meeting investors who were intrigued by the unproven but promising land of India. China was also catching the fancy of US investors, and many a delegation had travelled to the large semiconductor plant in Pudong district in Shanghai to experience the country's potential first-hand. Meanwhile, India had software product teams beginning to build new products out of Bangalore, instead of just following specifications from their US colleagues.

India and its billion people represented a virgin opportunity. Our pitches had borne fruit. Investors with long time horizons had chosen to back us with their capital. Capital that we would deploy in promising start-ups. Capital that would accelerate growth and help build industry leaders. The fundraise culminated rather quickly once our first few investors came in. These investors, known as LPs or 'limited partners', were taking a call based on our thesis, team strength and credibility. Overarching all this was their openness to India.

Our maiden fund was ready for deployment in May 2006. We had raised a cool $140 million and were ready to start. In June 2006, we formally opened for business.

Ashish Gupta and I moved from Silicon Valley to India. Ashish moved to Bangalore. He and Kanwaljit Singh would work out of our Bangalore office. Sanjeev Agarwal and I would work out of our Gurgaon office.

It had been a month since I moved back to India after spending seven years in Silicon Valley, Palo Alto, and I was just getting re-adjusted to a new way of life. Delhi wasn't home and the peculiarities of Delhi life were just revealing themselves to me. It was frustrating to see how people said they were going to do something 'now', but that didn't mean the present. It just meant sometime in the near future, and they called it 'now'. We would earnestly wait for delivery people, electricians and plumbers to show up and then actually get frustrated over the shoddiness and work ethic. Living in the US had conditioned us to expect predictable outcomes. After returning to Delhi, it took us a few years to change our habit of linking work to a timeline. It would happen, at some time in the future. Letting go of the 'when?' question was the path to nirvana.

Delhi was a city under construction. India was a country that was building highways for Ferraris as well as for 'jugaad rickshaws'. Several life-changing infrastructure projects like the national highway connecting Delhi to Gurgaon were still under construction. Stuck in a sea of cars for hours, I often had the urge to jump out and run to my destination through the maze of vehicles. At other times, I would imagine a large rocket-mounted car that could blow a tunnel through the gridlock. Sometimes I would drive myself crazy thinking about my car getting scraped by the road warriors around me. In those days, I would have no other choice but to sit and meditate. I needed to meditate to stay calm. No wonder India is called the land that draws out your spiritual self.

My kids, who were one and five years old respectively, had frequent heat-induced nosebleeds and stomach infections on their path to building their immunity. My wife was under pressure too, dealing with these health issues and trying to recreate some semblance of the life we had led in Palo Alto. We tried to create a warm cocoon of a familiar corner in a big, unfriendly city. One of the first things I did was get a fast Internet plan (at the time, it was Airtel EDGE) for my BlackBerry. I wanted to be connected at all times. It brought the comfort of instant access to work emails in my palm. But it also continued the long cycle of distractions and reduction of focus that I grappled with for many years. My wife would often remind me about my compulsive BlackBerry use, even in the delivery room, moments after our first child was born.

In our first month of existence as a venture fund, we were introduced to a company called MakeMyTrip. My partner had personally invested in the company and this relationship got us an entry pass to engage.

The traditional world of booking a flight ticket was an operational quagmire. The customer had to dial a call centre. The agent would ask for details like boarding airport, destination, name and class, and provide airline options. The calls would be long and often inconclusive. Mistakes were common and expensive.

With only 20 million Internet users in India, and the concept of e-tickets yet to emerge in 2006, MakeMyTrip was leading a slow train of modernization. Until more and more consumers chose the DIY route to booking tickets, MakeMyTrip looked doomed to operational hell.

Our local presence and a stated goal to help our investee companies were the main factors that drew MakeMyTrip towards us; it was going through growth pangs and needed investors who could help it overcome this friction. Operations were becoming a bottleneck to growth and had to be redrawn from scratch.

MakeMyTrip was on its second lease of life after the 2001 dotcom bust. Deep Kalra, co-founder of MakeMyTrip, had skilfully manoeuvred the company back from near-death, keeping the lights on using earnings from ticket sales to the expat Indian community. Educated in a Jesuit school in Delhi, Delhi University and then IIM Ahmedabad, Deep was intense, yet had the nonchalance of the privileged. He usually dressed in khakis and button-downs and was attentive and respectful to everyone around the table. We had several common friends from his school and neighbourhood. He had been an accomplished table tennis player in school and many of my friends who had played against him remembered his competitiveness.

Deep had started MakeMyTrip during the dotcom bubble of 2000. It was now six years old. He had seen the original exuberance wither away with the dotcom crash, investor interest wane and then disappear, and the company survive a near-death experience.

In 2005, he had raised fresh funding and was back to his original plan—an online travel agency where Internet-savvy travellers could book flight tickets.

Deep's early failure with MakeMyTrip had battle-hardened him. It had instilled in him the confidence that was required for the long-term nature of company building. He started his entrepreneurial journey selling bowling alleys in India—creating a new market, selling to local business owners and recovering payments. Not for the faint of heart.

At that time, MakeMyTrip operated from an office perched over a busy intersection in south Delhi with almost no parking space. My visits usually ended with a high degree of stress and eventual release as I finally managed to fit my car into a narrow slot, wedged between concrete pillars down a steep ramp.

My partners, Ashish and Kanwal, had come from Bangalore to join Sanjeev and me for a day-long meeting with the team at MakeMyTrip. In the early evening, we convened at the Sheraton Hotel over glasses of fresh juice and a fancy serving of brewed tea—it came with a timer. We were also on a tight leash where time was concerned. We had to move quickly on the decision. The team was only the four of us and we had full quorum. We chatted about how to structure the round, and more importantly, how to build comfort around the valuation that Deep expected for this round. While none of us could see the eventual height that the company would reach, we all felt we would be able to make attractive returns from its success.

Our temporary office was in a business centre in Gurgaon. We were waiting it out as our permanent office was in a building under construction. We expected to stay in the business centre for a year. It had a shared reception and charged for everything, like a low-cost airline. Our individual rooms were scattered around the labyrinthine floor. In the initial days, it was easy to forget the locations of the other rooms. It also felt cut off from the rest of the world. Gurgaon was a remote city, with most offices used by exiles from Delhi or low rent seekers.

Navigating a two-hour Delhi–Gurgaon commute and sitting in a windowless room felt like a forced exile as well. We were away from the daily chatter and mind-energizing meetings with start-ups. Thankfully, the MakeMyTrip transaction was keeping the action going for me, and Deep was an honourable opponent to grapple with.

The round was split three ways between SAIF, an existing investor in MakeMyTrip, Sierra Ventures, a well-known firm from Silicon Valley, and Helion. Deep was affable and knew exactly what he wanted in the negotiations. While he was intimately familiar with the minutest details in the legal agreements, he negotiated keeping the big picture in mind and was quick to move forward.

When the process of investment in a company begins, somehow, the world conspires to shake off the conviction. As we negotiated the agreements, we kept hearing about the terrible experiences many of our friends went through while booking tickets with MakeMyTrip. It was one of the first experiences of witnessing household conversations about a company that we were about to back.

Sierra had the longest timelines and the rest of us had to wait for them to figure out their first India investment. So the transaction proceeded in fits and starts and caused a fair degree of frustration on the unbelievably slow path to completion. My partners wondered if I was moving fast enough, and I had no option but to call the Sierra folks to check on their progress. Deep was keen to have a Silicon Valley brand so we all developed the patience needed to delink activity from timeline, although this time the source for the delay was not in India but surprisingly in Silicon Valley.

MakeMyTrip would eventually list on NASDAQ in 2010. It raised $70 million in its initial public offering (IPO) and was valued at $450 million. In 2017, MakeMyTrip was worth $3 billion.

The show must go online!

We shared our business centre office with several companies in the garment sourcing business who worked on behalf of foreign brands. We often shared elevator space with stacks of fabric samples. Every elevator ride was a reminder of how far I had come from Silicon Valley and how different India had become over the seven years that I had been away.

Standing in a corner of the elevator, with sweaty, underpaid employees cursing long commutes on motorbikes, carrying 50 kg fabric samples around Delhi and cheerfully going through the day was the ultimate India paradox. Here we were, a $140 million fund focused on tech-enabled businesses in a country that clearly had a lot of demand but no infrastructure and no pre-existing automation to build smarter businesses. Either we could look only for neat, self-sufficient businesses that added a layer on top of existing infrastructure but didn't need large amounts of cash, or find businesses that solved large, deep-rooted problems. The latter had to build infrastructure that wasn't there and so consumed gobs of capital. People mattered a lot more than servers in India. It would be decades before digitization replaced human-led processes.

Summer was over. Sierra had finally ironed out their issues and the MakeMyTrip round was done and dusted. Helion had invested $6 million. We were ready for more.

The 2006 Delhi winter was finally setting in after the chaos caused by the monsoon. The VC business is a bit like the monsoon—unpredictable and with uneven distribution. In this business, if you stay around long enough, you realize that while building a history of triumphs is rare, a history of misses is definitely guaranteed. In the winter of 2006, I missed two companies that went on to make a big mark in the Indian start-up scene.

These companies had appointed bankers to help them raise capital, and both sides had followed totally opposite approaches. The first was a Mumbai-based company called BookMyShow. BookMyShow was the only online ticketing company for movie tickets in India. It had a nice ring to it. Every seat in a theatre was part of a perishable inventory, like a flight ticket. If you could make it easy for moviegoers to pick and book their seats in advance, it would help sell more seats and improve the moviegoing experience.

The banker emailed us a lengthy document about the business and its prospects. This document, called the private placement memorandum or PPM for short, was sixty pages long. It had reams of information. A banker would usually sit with the company management for weeks to understand the business and prepare a document with that level of detail. It required converting the future of the business into a series of financial projections. I was intrigued by the detailed PPM and wanted to give it a thorough read. I printed the sixty pages, closed the door of my office and settled down to go over the rows upon rows of business descriptions and dozens of tables of numbers. The cover had the official name 'Bigtree Entertainment' in bold on it. My mind wandered a few times, thanks to my compulsive habit of staring at my BlackBerry, but somehow, before the end of the day, I had trudged through to the end of the PPM.

There is an archaic law in India about movie ticket sales being restricted to the theatre's box office. This was the only constraint in an otherwise digitally neat business. To access the seat inventory, BookMyShow had sold to theatres a software that they had sourced from a New Zealand–based company. This software helped theatres with seat allocation but also gave unique inventory access to BookMyShow. BookMyShow used this access as a competitive edge to build a consumer-facing business. It was a straight enough business model, and being a movie buff myself I could understand the power of a single source of all movie tickets. The niggling doubt was: how badly did I want a confirmed ticket in hand before I went to the theatre? Did the average customer care enough?

The company had shown remarkable promise in aggregating the supply of seats in various movie theatres. It could potentially sit on this inventory as a single source. At that time, there were fewer multiplexes and more single-screen theatres. Chains like PVR were not as common as they are today. The supply seemed fragmented. The aggregator could have become very powerful.

The founder, Ashish Hemrajani, was young, suave and passionate about his vision. Ashish and I met in my office along with their banker. Ashish, like Deep, was born into a privileged household and had taken to entrepreneurship early. He was a man on a mission and had a youthful exuberance about him. And boy, could he talk! I thought his Mumbai upbringing had something to do with this deep-seated belief that movies were an integral part of entertainment for every Indian. Ashish was almost gleeful when he walked me through his journey and his plans. He had travelled a meaningful distance without a serious backer. By rolling revenue back into the business, and with private capital from his family and friends, he had centred his life on the creation of BookMyShow. He and his co-founders had started the company in 1999. And like MakeMyTrip, they had kept the lights on through the seven long years of the funding winter. Finally, VCs had reappeared in India and there was a justifiable expectation of fresh funding.

The best part of BookMyShow's model was its simplicity. It was a low-margin business but the number of people who would eventually buy movie tickets on the Internet was projected to grow by many thousands in the future. The tough times that followed the founding years of BookMyShow were not just due to lack of money, but also competition. Eventually, BookMyShow won both battles. Many competitors perished. BookMyShow was more or less the last company standing, and like MakeMyTrip, it dominated the online movie ticketing market.

Ashish had the pulse of both sides of the business: the consumer-facing side and the part that aggregated tickets across movie theatres all over the country. The founding team was a classic Silicon Valley–style ensemble of a tight-knit group of people focused on technology and business.

A role that was a fixture in any Silicon Valley start-up was that of the product head. The product head was the bridge between the customer and the engineering team. The role required the product manager to translate between these two functions. This ensured that engineering built great features that made production adoption easy.

This role had still not appeared in consumer Internet companies in India, and as expected, it was missing in both

MakeMyTrip and BookMyShow. When the need for it came up in conversation with Ashish, his response revealed the general absence of people who could fill this role in India.

In 2007, my view of the Internet market in India was shaped by constraining factors like the lack of broadband infrastructure. There just wasn't enough Internet access. There was a sense of despondency about the lack of devices, of deep-pocketed service providers and even of reasons to go online for the mass user. Our internal thesis was that Internet users would grow steadily but slowly. Companies that were relying on online users for growth needed to budget for many more years to get to their goals.

This outlook was the premise we operated from when we looked at consumer Internet businesses in 2006. In the case of BookMyShow, their revenue model was based on a commission of Rs 10 per ticket to be paid by theatre owners for every ticket sold. My main worry was the size of the revenue that BookMyShow could get to. I was thinking that in a small user market, a small commission would build a small company.

So with Ashish, our discussions kept revolving around the size of the market. This was one question for which there were no easy answers. No one had seen the future. Even if the future unfolded slowly, I could not see either fast market adoption or market factors of movie ticket commissions increasing.

MakeMyTrip operated in the same market, but there we could see the work-around that consumers were doing to obtain an essential service. An airline ticket represented travel, which denoted a high priority. This was a necessary spend. People in

India love movies, but would they ever worry about buying movie tickets in advance because prices would otherwise go up or seats would run out? Or would neighbourhood stores set up computers and provide movie-ticket-buying as a service to their shoppers? The answer in my head was 'not so sure'.

So, after perching myself on the safe seat of logical reasoning, I concluded that this was not an investment we wanted to make. We conveyed our decision to Ashish. I was wrong about the market size, of course. BookMyShow went from strength to strength and raised Rs 150 crore from SAIF Partners. The market did not grow. The market exploded! BookMyShow sold 100 million tickets in 2016. In January 2018, reports indicated that Ashish was raising another round of funding and investors had valued the company at over Rs 3000 crore. Ouch!

The karma of Vijay Shekhar Sharma before Paytm

In 2007, the Indian market had several vacuums—the vacuum of Internet users, the vacuum of devices like laptops and smartphones, and the vacuum of infrastructure around delivery and payments. As investors, we could afford to make choices and use logic to predict markets. But entrepreneurs were like the Argonauts who had set sail in a foggy sea. They had to keep their faith alive every day to keep looking for the land that eluded them. They were not timing the market. They had to use every tailwind to move faster. When the 'timing was right', they would take off like a rocket and many people would mistake their persistence for luck.

In November 2006, a director in the corporate finance team of a Big Four accounting firm wanted us to meet a young entrepreneur called Vijay Shekhar Sharma. Vijay was operating a company called One97 out of an office space in Nehru Place, a business district in south Delhi. The banker and Vijay had a common friend from their engineering college days and this was more a favour than a typical assignment.

Vijay had given a minority ownership of One97 to a private investor to get started. He had been in the market for additional financing for a long time. Some shady operators gave him the runaround with a promise of debt but nothing had materialized. The clock was ticking and this delay was stretching his patience and deepening his desperation. Not until his friend connected him to this banker was Vijay aware of a rare animal called venture capital. The banker felt the environment had become conducive to venture financing. He got Vijay to start doing the rounds at various VC firms, including Helion.

Accompanied by the banker, Vijay came to meet us in our office. They drove up from Vijay's rented flat in south Delhi in his Maruti 800. The first thing about Vijay that caught my attention, even before his first words registered in my brain, was his absolute self-assurance.

One97 had a grand vision of owning a network of servers across telecom networks. This network would feed paid content to millions of subscribers for a share of the revenue. So far so good.

Vijay's ambition was to become a dominant player in the telecom market by not only owning content but also having the ability to deliver it. He spotted a gap—telecom companies were willing to share revenue with him as long as he undertook the cost of building this content delivery network. Owning and operating a network of servers required an upfront investment of millions of dollars. The servers were meant to be his weapons and would drive the next wave of content consumption on feature phones. Once installed in the network, these servers would act as gatekeepers for anyone who wanted to monetize their content. So Vijay was going to ram in all he could, in every telecom network, in every telecom company.

Vijay's voice was high-pitched. Unlike pitches which ramble on to produce a soporific effect, Vijay's incantations kept my brain on edge. Unlike the typical mould of savvy entrepreneurs who pitched to us, Vijay did not have an Ivy League or multinational corporation background. He was a small-town guy, like me. But the similarity ended there. I had gone to a Jesuit school where the emphasis on speaking proper English had been drilled into my head. Vijay was speaking in a curious Hinglish. He punctuated every sentence with an 'okay'. But damn, he had some energy. I could tell that sitting down was too passive for him. Given a chance, he would stand up and walk all over the room while explaining himself. His hands had a life of their own. As he moved them, the vision of Vijay Shekhar Sharma started getting painted in my head.

He had me in goosebumps during the course of this first meeting.

We followed up with a few more meetings to understand the business better. Vijay did not have a telecom background but as a vendor to them he had developed a strong sense of the commercialism required in this business. His business was a mix of the hard elements, negotiating deals with telecom giants, and the soft aspect of producing entertainment for consumers. Not surprisingly, the aspect he spoke about least was the content itself. His approach to content was limited to what One97 could produce internally. As investors, it was apparent to us that Vijay's focus was on scale and competitive barriers. If he had been passionate about sourcing the hottest content coming out of Bollywood, we would have been worried about his business sense. According to Vijay, he would work with content generation companies and not take the creative risk himself. He was here to own the distribution of content to telecom subscribers.

We visited Vijay's office. It was located in the heart of Nehru Place, an area that hosted many trading businesses, and where business meant selling.

The fifth floor office brought some of the Nehru Place buzz to the inside. Across the length of the office walls were windows that looked upon the busy Ring Road. Traffic crawled below us.

Almost chaotic, every square inch of space had been assigned to driving revenue. You could see that people working here were not seasoned engineers, but executives building a company of the future. They were fixing problems of today and earning revenue for the day. There were no ping-pong tables and X-boxes to provide relief during long nights of coding. These guys were here to cut deals, run operations and sell. The astrologers preparing predictions for mobile users sat next to network engineers. Under one roof, on one floor, about seventy-five people were delivering the daily fix of horoscopes, sports scores, jokes and movie songs. Anything audio or text, anything that you could listen to or read, was being produced.

To get a 360-degree view of the criss-crossing functional and organizational lines running through the company, we met members of Vijay's core team. This was a start-up team that rallied around its leader. Vijay's energy was clearly spent signing up telecom companies. He was nothing if not driven. To support the bold vision, the operating plan was broken down carrier by carrier and some clear short-term goals were identified. Vijay would have given an arm and a leg to sign up MTNL, the government-owned carrier. Focus on one big win at a time. This was a fantastic revelation—Vijay was focused on tangible achievements.

To cross-check Vijay's plan, we spoke to seasoned executives in large telecom companies, some of whom were One97's customers. The response was by and large in favour of One97. Not owning their network was not uncommon for telcos, but these companies were massive. Their gargantuan sizes could consume several One97s before breakfast. The commercial departments of these telecom companies are notorious for breaking vendors down one rupee at a time. And in 2006, of course, no one anticipated the smartphone tsunami. Content-rich smartphones would make One97's business redundant as consumers would slowly stop purchasing content from the operators.

In all our interactions, Vijay's raw energy would cloud the nuances of an investor conversation. We still struggled to distil his passionate pitches and assess his ability to build a scalable organization, hire talent from the telecom world and build a predictable business. After much internal debate, we decided to call Vijay in to present to Helion's team. This usually meant that we were reaching the end of our diligence and were ready to make up our mind. Our debate revolved around the challenges of building a valuable business with customers who were programmed to reduce costs and had armies of people to beat down rates. We took comfort in the installations that Vijay had already done and a business model that was off the ground.

Besides myself, only one of my partners had met Vijay previously. I didn't know what to expect from the presentation. Would his impassioned delivery cause confusion or convey the business value? Would we be able to come to a consensus or would we struggle for more inputs?

Vijay and the banker sputtered up again from Delhi in the blue Maruti 800.

Our temporary office in the business centre had a large U-shaped table. I had prepared my partners to expect an unconventional founder. Vijay was in the centre pit and he chose to pace around the open space. With both hands waving and his trademark soprano voice, he commanded our full attention. Pausing only to catch his breath, Vijay came across as a force of nature.

In addition to his punctuations of 'okay', he would provide a translation in Hindi of whatever he had just said. The banker was gambling on this display to floor a room full of investors. Vijay was able to balance out the unknown with his display of confidence and hunger to succeed. Within an hour, this thirty-two-year-old from Aligarh had not only floored a room full of VCs, but also generated some fondness for his classic David-versus-Goliath persona.

In the discussion that followed, our partnership was unanimous in considering One97 as a worthwhile play on the growth of content consumption by the fast-growing Indian telecom subscriber base. And in Vijay, we saw the promise of a new generation of entrepreneurs who were breaking the traditional mould. They didn't come with a background in the space they wanted to disrupt. They didn't come from posh schools or carry MBA degrees. They spoke 'Indian' and knew what it took to build Indian companies with desi sensibilities.

I put in a call to the banker and realized he had been trying to reach me as well. Vijay had presented at another VC firm and done an equally impressive job. We realized the other firm was ahead of us—they had already offered a term sheet and locked Vijay in, preventing him from talking to other investors. This was standard practice; we would have done the same. Life was not fair and great entrepreneurs didn't stay unclaimed for long. We had come to recognize the need to find a balance between an entrepreneur's understanding of an opportunity and our own. We also realized that all entrepreneurs were not articulate, but their ability to express their passion was not compromised by language, words or slick presentation material.

As it turned out, it would take Vijay one more attempt at company building to make us regret our miss even more. One97 had its share of challenges and headwinds. But then, nobody could have foreseen what Apple was planning to launch in the year of this discussion. The first-generation 4 GB iPhone came out exactly a year after our last meeting with Vijay, and the world was never the same again.

2

By late 2006, we had added a chief financial officer (CFO) and more staff to our two office locations in Gurgaon and Bangalore. Our Bangalore office was right next to a golf course and the airfield of Hindustan Aeronautics. The Bangalore airport was part of this airfield and was right in the middle of the city. Landing at the airport and getting to a meeting took less than thirty minutes. Suburbs like Whitefield were still home to only the brave and the lonely.

Our CFO, R. Natrajan, or Nats, as he was better known, had joined us from a software company. Nats was a full-charge battery who could chase open items ferociously to closure. High on action orientation, Nats would go through a steep learning curve and have his hands full over the next two years.

Our maiden investment in MakeMyTrip was done. We had begun helping them think about how to handle their customer support issues. Telephone-based ordering and paper tickets were adding orders, but customer complaints were harder to track and resolve.

India's Internet adoption challenge in 2006 was like the proverbial chicken-and-egg problem. Japan and Korea already had broadband speeds on phones that put the US mobile market to shame. Consumers in these markets were using early versions of smartphones. Companies like NTT and KDDI would write specific software for specific functions to run applications on phones.

There were 100 million mobile phones in India in 2006. Not smartphones, but feature phones. A Bangalore-based company, JiGrahak, was attempting to convert this large base of mobile users into millions of micro-transactions. We wrote our second cheque to JiGrahak as their first investor.

JiGrahak was building an application that allowed Indian consumers to use their mobile phones as transaction devices. As prosaic as it may sound now, it brought to life the original premise of transacting from a consumer's own device. Buying movie tickets, train tickets and mobile phone talktime, all from your personal handy device.

JiGrahak had a single founder: a twenty-nine-year-old first-time entrepreneur who came from a metal trading family. Long-haired, tall and with a slight beer belly, Saurabh was an early prototype of founders who brought technology and business-building skills together in a single package. He had a casual air about him, but possessed a sense of purpose and a clarity of vision that were rare in those days.

In the days when getting a basic mobile Internet connection was a uniquely challenging task for a consumer and the ability to pay from a mobile phone through an Internet gateway unheard of, JiGrahak had embarked on a very ambitious journey. The size of the challenge was massive. Essentially, JiGrahak was a marketplace on the mobile, or a 'supermarket', as Saurabh liked to call it. But the challenge of adding every merchant and processing every transaction was like pulling teeth. JiGrahak was solving complex engineering problems *and* driving customer usage at a time when burning cash to attract customers wasn't fashionable.

It needed millions of transactions to make the maths work, and 'millions of something' seemed like too long a shot in 2006. As is often the case, suspension of reality is required to appreciate the best-case scenario when you are sitting in that place and in that time. The prospect of millions of mobile phone consumers doing millions of transactions with thousands of merchants, each putting a tiny fee in JiGrahak's account, needed a big stretch of imagination. When e-commerce companies like Flipkart started in 2011, the same suspension of belief took place. A lot changed in India in those five years, as we later looked back and realized.

Just like Saurabh was among the first of the new entrepreneurs, JiGrahak was also a prototype of the kind of start-ups that would follow in the coming years in India—lean, product-oriented, custom-built and chasing an audacious goal.

The neighbourhood of Koramangala in Bangalore deserves the moniker of being the original 'garage' of India. Its houses have been nestling start-ups since the mid-nineties. One of the earlier investments I was involved with, Graycell, was one of the first to convert a large house surrounded by the generous Bangalore foliage into a twenty-four-hour, coffee-powered, sleep-in-office, 'wake up and code' den. Graycell was building a messaging network that strung together SMS delivery platforms for mobile operators around the globe—two-way messaging between any two mobile devices via the Internet.

Koramangala's lanes were quieter then and the neighbours were sympathetically supportive of the wildly ambitious young generation of entrepreneurs. Someone with the ambition of building consumer-focused start-ups was an even rarer commodity because, barring a few IT services start-ups, there was a paucity of role models, even in the US.

Almost a decade after I came across Graycell, I returned to Koramangala to visit JiGrahak. The employee count was less than twenty when we invested. Like most people who are able to see a market before time, Saurabh had to personally own his vision and constantly paint a picture of the future for others to see. The vision had to be sold to customers, partners and future employees. Being brave, ambitious and perhaps providing a window to the future allowed JiGrahak to have intrigue. The intrigue of a disrupter. Disruption leading to a big market. The promise of the unknown. For every dream seller, there is a dream buyer. People who would like to believe in your vision of change. Those who are equally tired of the old ways. JiGrahak was beginning to find these believers.

Like Deep Kalra, Saurabh also made it clear what help he needed from his VC firm. He wanted help with finding quality businesspeople to join his lean team of engineers. There were lots of partnerships to be done. This meant we were playing out our promise of being active investors. The second role of a VC was getting added to the plate—the duty of helping investee companies grow. The first duty was, of course, to find start-ups which demonstrated high reserves of potential energy that could be converted to kinetic energy.

In early 2007, we moved from our temporary space at a business centre to our new office in Gurgaon—a black granite office complex on Golf Course Road. Located in the same complex as the research centre of a German software company, it was a modern building that freed us from the frustrating obstacle of finding roadside parking every day.

It had a nice restaurant in the front lawn and a large, welcoming lobby. We shared elevator space with employees from DE Shaw and Merck. My parking slot was on the second basement, which one reached through a complicated maze of left and right turns through the two floors. I would be able to accomplish this manoeuvre with my eyes closed and within 52 seconds at the end of the twelve years I spent here.

Around the same time, the single greatest game-changer for India's tech ecosystem was announced by Steve Jobs. The first new iPhone was announced with much fanfare in January 2007. It would trigger Google to rush through to a beta release of Android later in the year. So much power in a little device in the palm of the consumer would be a seismic shift in how the Indian consumer would start consuming Internet services. The full impact of this launch would take at least five more years to transform the world's third-largest consumer market.

How the next two years panned out for us and for every other VC firm was unexpected in its pace and activity. Like us, many other VC firms in India were founded in 2006. Somehow, the size of the first fund for most firms was around $140 million. Investors in overseas countries who backed these funds found this to be a comfortable size for firms that had a team of two or three investment partners. Like us, most of these firms came back for their second fundraise in 2008. This meant that 2007 and 2008 were two of the most action-packed years for any VC investing in India. After a long, dry spell, Indian VC firms were making a new investment once in two months on average.

Newspapers understood that investment amounts quoted in rupees made for eye-catching headlines. Multinational executives quit their jobs to start new businesses. Many Indians living overseas came back to build cross-border businesses or solve India-specific problems. The surviving Indian start-ups from the 2001 dotcom boom came back to life. Universities set up centres for teaching entrepreneurship. Art funds were raised to generate returns from the increasing value of artwork. Real estate, infrastructure and movie funds joined the party. The Indian stock market was pumped up on global liquidity and doubled its value in twenty months.

Perched in our ninth-floor office, we got a bird's-eye view of the dust bowl of Gurgaon. A skyline that sprouted fresh towers every time you took your eyes off it. DLF, the largest developer in Gurgaon, had just completed the largest IPO in

Indian history and was rapidly changing the skyline with its newfound capital.

Our office was spacious and designed in muted shades with steel and glass finishes. Most visitors were impressed by its quality and neatness. About 4000 square feet for about six of us. My office overlooked the 150-million-year-old Aravali range. My view was an endless canopy of the thorny *keekar* or Mexican mesquite, a non-native dominant tree that prevented any form of biodiversity. But green nevertheless.

With start-ups recognizing us as investors who were seriously engaged and deploying capital, what started off was a deluge of new proposals. The availability of capital had prompted a rush of start-ups created by first-time entrepreneurs. Most of these entrepreneurs had not experienced a start-up environment because it did not exist. We started receiving twenty or more new plans a week to evaluate. Between the four of us, we had five new plans to process every week. We needed new hands on deck to help us handle the flow. A search for people to join the team was initiated.

The quandary of being an investor in India in 2007 was that the gaps were so many that it was easy to pick a problem area to solve. They all seemed large. But while the demand was high and the product and quality of the team made sense, there was no ability to predict the timing of when Indian consumers would get online. You could enter a company and sit there waiting for the market to arrive. When would enough Indians get online? The US market seemed very distant. Facebook was adding users like no other Internet company had done before.

It had added 8 million users in the first three months of 2007. Comparatively, active Internet users in all of India increased by 1.5 million in the same period to reach 28 million.

One day I found in my inbox a proposal from a company I knew from my days in college. I have a picture of myself holding a copy of their thick Delhi yellow pages book when I was in my final year at BITS, Pilani.

Getit was already twenty years old in 2007. It had a top accounting firm representing it to raise capital. Everything about it was screaming unconventional, challenging and unproven. This was a company that could place itself between the oncoming adoption of online access to Google and how Indians were expected to access information for local businesses using voice. Somewhere in the slide deck, the plan to build a mobile-phone-based search for local information was also mentioned.

Around the same time, a friend referred to us a two-founder team carrying a paper plan. The founding team, one of whom was American and the other Indian, had law degrees and had worked as lawyers. US firms paid out billions of dollars to US law firms every year. There was room to create a new service provider that could outsource some of that work to India and deliver services at lower costs. We were aware of this trend but had not found a suitable company that we felt could build this into a scale business. We felt that most teams either lacked a true understanding of customer pain or were happy to build a commodity business that competed only on lower price.

This business, called UnitedLex, was so early that it had neither a team nor any customers, but the founders displayed a solid understanding of how US enterprises were thinking of lowering their legal costs. UnitedLex was an opportunity to exploit early a large market opportunity with a credible team that intimately knew the needs of the North American large customer. One of the top-tier VC firms in India had already invested in a similar company and they had wanted us to invest along with them.

Our belief was that the market was large enough to accommodate more than one large company. The CEO, Dan, had worked in an outsourced company and was aware of how to build a cross-border company. He preferred to dress up in formal suits and lived in Florida. His father was a surgeon who had treated the mother of a famous Bollywood actor, and Dan's early experience of India was when he had been hosted by the actor's father in his Mumbai home.

Dan and his co-founder had been working together in an Indian outsourcing company and had been exploring the legal services space. During one of our meetings with them, one of the co-founders started an edgy argument with the other co-founder. It was awkward for us to watch such disagreements being laid out in the open.

Getit and UnitedLex both represented compelling market opportunities.

Getit's plan was to transform the revenue-generating yellow pages business into a voice search business, using the underlying assets of data on local businesses. Would the company whose consumers earlier flipped through dog-eared volumes of yellow pages be able to transform itself significantly to seek more dynamic information using a more scale medium . . . like . . . like a phone call? With a call to a catchy number with an easy-to-remember sequence? And with every call, the merchant who was discovered would pay a commission against the business that Getit drove. Plausible, right?

Now for the challenge, the unconventional and the unproven.

The challenge, of course, would be to have enough information to compel the consumer to make a habit of calling Getit's toll-free number. This would be possible only if Getit could answer most calls satisfactorily. Many calls would have to be to provide general information like hospital numbers without any money being made. The rest had to be calls to merchants who had already signed up or could be sold to. A business that supported nationwide sales, a database of phone numbers that frequently needed updating, and yet was inextricably tied to its twenty-year-old business. A sales force that was used to conventional products and carrying a rate chart that was not linked to measuring results.

It was unconventional because it was family-run. A prominent family that had multiple branches and cross-holdings and came with the trappings of legacy. The son of the founder had taken over with the promise of building a new business and the recognition that the traditional business was beginning to decline.

And it was unproven because technology underpinning was not the strong point of a yellow pages business. Selling ads and printing books were. Is technology a piece of genetic code that can be inserted into the DNA or is it too core to the company's approach to how a problem can be solved? Does it define culture or can it thrive when confined only to a room or a floor in the office?

Getit had operations in twenty cities, a 500-strong workforce and a revenue of Rs 60 crore. UnitedLex existed mostly on a paper plan.

For the UnitedLex investment, our decision-making relied heavily on referencing the founders, the potential customers and the plan. The UnitedLex founders had met at another outsourcing company where they got to know each other and decided to step out to start off on their own. The chemistry between them was not obvious. Dan was clinical and his co-founder was a provocateur, a challenger who questioned the norm. They sometimes started arguing in the middle of meetings.

We decided to do a deep dive into their background. On the customer side, Dan had arranged a call with the general counsel at a Fortune 100 company. I had to first set the context of why the call was so important for us. With some coaxing, the general counsel shared with me how his budget was under pressure. His company's board was questioning his department's spend. Other large departments like finance, customer support and technical support had already shown cost reductions by offshoring. This was the common message from all the general counsels we spoke to. The call revealed the layers of outsourcing already occurring in the legal space to US-based services companies. The need to hire lawyers who could understand and manage legal contracts was an expense even the largest US corporates were keen to lower, even if it meant sending confidential contracts to offices in India.

At Getit, we started our round of meetings with the founders, Sidharth and his father, Rameshji.

The meetings with the management were held at the family's office near the 'press row' of Delhi. The newspaper offices and the printing presses were all within a mile's radius. The building was chock-full of people but like any other Delhi office space, it was decaying after years of half-hearted maintenance. The Getit office interiors were dimly lit with the seventies' Formica design. Recently refurbished spaces alternated with what must have been the original interiors from twenty years ago. Spending on upgrades had been diverted to select areas. A hodge-podge of the old and the new, the privileged and the deprived.

The family was warm and gracious. The tea service, which included cashews and almonds, was clearly reserved for special meetings. The son who was taking over from the father was well-versed in the nuances of yellow pages and clued in to developments in search and technology. Moreover, he emphatically projected the new direction as the only direction.

Our discussions went on for months. We felt the need to be comfortable about the culture and intention. When a family business has to be tweaked and eventually killed, most owners would flinch. The Getit family spanned generations and they had to unwind and clean up decades of relationships. The family's commitment was visible in their actions. They had consolidated all their eggs in the Getit basket. As shareholders, we would be on the same side. The risk we would need to digest would be the family transforming the business by launching a new product, proving its utility to merchants and rolling it out across the twenty markets that they were already operating their books business in.

At UnitedLex, now convinced about the business potential, we moved on to what is called 'referencing the founders'. The founders would provide a list of people that could offer their views on their personality and capability. VCs would then call the people on that list but would also find some people who were not on the list. Speaking to ten to fifteen people to understand the past is not uncommon. The disagreements that we had witnessed in our previous meetings were still rankling us.

We concluded that with their background, the founders lacked the competency to build and run a large delivery centre. Their roles were complementary and my partner and I classified them in the roles of the creator and the destroyer from Hindu mythology. We saw destruction as an equally valuable activity in a start-up's journey. It would help UnitedLex break down the complex needs of its customers into a process that could be delivered from India.

The customer calls were encouraging; an anchor customer seemed likely as soon as we had invested and the company had the funds to deliver services.

We decided to go ahead with UnitedLex, putting $2 million in a new, unproven company. There was no pressure to add additional investors but we were joined by two angel investors with very strong credentials in outsourcing. Dealing with lawyers who were also founders was both a boon and a bane in working through the legal contracts. The UnitedLex co-founder who led the negotiations was convinced that our lawyer didn't know how to draft legal agreements.

What should have been a simple first round of financing was a drama of epic proportions. Our lawyers presented the company with a first draft of the lengthy agreement called the Shareholders Agreement, the SHA for short. After UnitedLex went through the SHA, a frustrated cry of disbelief went up. They thought the SHA draft was a piece of shit. I got a call from the co-founder. You need to immediately fire your law firm, he said. The partner who is talking to us doesn't know how to even draft. And don't even mention the abilities of the associate in the law firm. I was yet to figure out that this sort of extreme views would be the opening lines of many other conversations that would follow. I am a good listener, but a good listener needs to dispel notions. I laid out my sympathies but ended the call with a fait accompli. The law firm would stay. We have got to live with our displeasures.

There was so much we were all going to learn. I had to develop the patience of a fisherman and the listening ability of a counsellor.

Negotiating the legal agreement at Getit was extraordinarily lengthy as the family felt vulnerable at losing 100 per cent control. Every point was negotiated over weeks. The biggest fear we were dealing with was the eventuality that we may sell our shareholding to a competitive company, upsetting the balance. Night after night, we would sit down for long, never-ending phone calls that would be inconclusive. I would usually be tearing my hair out at our misplaced consumption of energy because I felt that all this time and effort would be better spent building the product and getting users. Lengthy negotiations are not only unproductive in the venture business but also risky because either side can find options or go through a rethink.

Usually, the test of a long relationship is surviving tough periods and coming out as friends. Getit's founder Sidharth would address me as 'Rahulji'. He masterfully disguised the urgency that any founder would have to bring in fresh capital so that his position wasn't weakened. Sidharth and I would often threaten each other that we would walk out of the transaction. But we would both promptly come back to the negotiating table.

After establishing a new record for the time taken to finalize a single investment, Helion presented a Rs 20 crore check to Getit.

Our portfolio for our first fund had grown rapidly. Our stated focus was to invest in tech-enabled companies that were using technology to deliver a new service but not building technology for technology's sake. We believed that the opportunity lay in businesses that served global enterprises and domestic consumers.

In 2006, we had made four new investments, and in 2007, we made another eight. Our investments had variety. A team of four investment partners was chasing unique themes and the final portfolio was not showing an easily discernible pattern.

One of the investments was in a chain of beauty salons called YLG or You Look Great. Often, the joke that accompanied the name was, do 'you look great' before or after the treatment? It served only women and its first market was Bangalore. The founder had built a similar business for a large retail group. YLG marked our first investment where the role of tech was minimal. It only made sense because in the universe of beauty salons in India, there was room to create a new brand. The country was on a secular growth path, economic growth was percolating to the middle class, and with their prosperity, people wanted to look good to feel good. We also invested in what was a precursor to the 'shared economy', HummingBird, a business that allowed property owners to put out their free space on rent for business travellers. A HummingBird apartment was a homestay that provided a uniform experience across all its properties. It was never marketed as a consumer brand and tied up with corporates for the short-term stay needs of their junior employees.

Founders reimagine the world all the time. They do not budget for timing as much as VCs do. In some way, basic ideas do not change. Better connectivity with our environment, ubiquitous communication with friends and strangers, feeling good about ourselves, and 'cheaper and better' are ideas that work across the ages. In another decade, a Graycell could have grown like WhatsApp, a JiGrahak like Paytm, but there is such a vast difference in outcome in seemingly similar concepts. The constant analysis of what makes some start-ups successful while some equally smart founders fail shows that timing has a massive role. This one factor is a huge determinant of success and is hardest to determine.

With twelve investments done from our first fund, we had to go back to raising our next fund. The global economic environment was going down fast. Several scary moments had already been registered through 2007 in the US economy. That's where the bulk of our investors resided. 2008 was opening even worse than expected. Perched atop a precipice, the US housing market was staring down a crevasse. Home prices had started falling and the US Fed started 2008 by lowering interest rates to boost demand, but the problem lay far deeper.

Further into the year, September 2008 would put brakes on investor interest not only for India but also for private investments. In September 2008, the US Congress would reject Ben Bernanke's bailout bill, and the US market would swiftly drop to half from its high point a year before. Asset managers who had earlier invested in venture funds would struggle to maintain a balance between their liquid investments in public stock and illiquid investments in private equity (PE). With public holdings losing value, the re-allocation would mean cutting back on PE exposure. We were hearing that fund managers who were investing in VCs were down by an average 25 per cent in value. Many took fatal blows. Teams churned.

In troubled times, when economic strain is so widespread, even the best of VC funds struggle to raise additional capital. But our timing worked well this time. We were in and out before the real panic set in. We closed our second fund in April 2008 and were back in the middle of the start-up frenzy in India.

3

India has had three distinct periods in the evolution of its venture ecosystem. It started in 1997 with two internationally oriented Silicon Valley firms setting up India-focused funds—Draper International and Walden International. I was the first employee of Walden India. Walden was coming off its success in Singapore and Taiwan. In 1997, India was just a large country with a foreign-capital-friendly policy, not the third-largest consumer market in the world that it is now. The IT revolution had not taken place and no shoots of the new-age economy were sprouting yet. The founders of Flipkart and Paytm were still wrapping up high school. Looking back on this first period feels like *Back to the Future*—where the concept of venture capital was coming from Silicon Valley but seemed alien to the Indian entrepreneur.

Walden invested in a company founded by media mogul Ronnie Screwvala called Teleshopping Network or TSN. TSN was a telesales company that used the power of TV programming (as it was then called) to solve India's retail gap. With Ronnie Screwvala's strength in video production, TSN was able to create a dent in the telesales space and came of age when its uniquely sourced product, the Roti Maker, became a hit. The excitement of phones ringing on the order floor sent hearts racing. Sales depended on variables like the duration of the demo video and the likeability of the personality demonstrating the product on the TV show. I would hang out at the TSN offices, understanding the science of roti making and also the shipping challenges and cash collection challenges in India in 1998. A fun ride all considered, but the company never made it.

The VC boat in India was still looking for the wind in its sails despite the Internet boom in Silicon Valley. Yahoo and Netscape had gone public by 1996. A few pioneers like Ajit Balakrishnan and Sanjeev Bikhchandani had exploited the power of the Internet. The Rediff.com domain was registered in India in 1996 while Naukri.com was launched in 1997.

The second period started around 1999. Domestic funds like WestBridge and ChrysCapital were launched. Companies like eGurucool, Jobsahead and Indya.com were founded by young founders and, of course, MakeMyTrip appeared on the scene in 2000. This activity was asphyxiated by the dotcom bust in the US. I moved to Silicon Valley and witnessed the triage in VC portfolios, the arrival of the nuclear winter in VC Land and the subsequent company shutdowns, lease breakages and bankruptcies.

India's start-up ecosystem, which was still germinating, was put in cold storage. Investment firms either shut down or made the incredibly successful move to public equities.

2006 marked the year when several new VC firms were founded, mostly by ex-entrepreneurs. Their investors were long-term ones like university endowments. Together, they created a vibrant, active ecosystem that picked up steam from 2012 onwards.

This period in 2006 was unique for India because, in collective action, a large number of the most credible investors in VC came together to back VC funds in India. This was the most high-quality capital because it came with the experience and the patience needed to understand the on-ground reality.

The same set of investors also backed funds in China at the same time. These investors realized the need for local funds run with local understanding as a better option than foreign funds, which would fly to India to do occasional deals.

In 2006, India's attraction was not yet clear. It had the potential to create technology because of the huge base of tech talent. But was there a large local market in which valuable companies could be built? Was there enough start-up talent? In the venture capital timeline, six years means two funds—that's how many can be raised and deployed in that period. This meant that sophisticated investors in VC funds would have more than sufficient data on how successful their bet on India turned out by 2012.

Our second fund was closed in 2008. It was raised from almost the same set of backers as the first fund. It was larger, and since then, we had added one more investment professional. Now we were a team of seven investment professionals. That needed more formal coordination across two offices.

Our weekly Monday calls were productive in having group discussions around shortlisted deals. We started a quarterly review to discuss the portfolio and get a perspective on our progress as a group. We would prepare for the quarterly meetings with an update of the last quarter broken into 'hits' and 'misses'. While it was naturally hard to discuss the misses openly, this was a valuable exercise. Discussing our misses as a group helped us develop the habit of breaking bad news fast and helped bring honesty into the conversation.

It also helped us channelize resources to the portfolio. Does a company need sales help? Does it need better financial support? Does it need help hiring a special resource? Define the problem and use the group's resources to come up with the solution. After the initial investment, building a strong company was a group task. We had to tap into the best possible internal or external resource.

Meanwhile, my kids had adapted well and the Delhi to Gurgaon commute had been eased with the National Highway work completed. I could now relax through the car rides, be more productive and think more. But as an investor newly responsible for deploying other people's money into my recommended investment, I found myself often overcome with frustration and fear of failure and my inability to act soon enough. I had so much riding on the performance of the start-ups I backed that my life started revolving entirely around them. A year would wrap up in four quarters, but unlike a founder's life, which had intermittent periods of highs and lows, a VC like me, who looked for highs in his portfolio's performance, had a long wait ahead. This was a delayed gratification business all right, but how delayed, I had no way of knowing. The highs were short-lived, but every time a company hit a speed breaker, I would become stressed about the long-term outlook. My family was not taking well to my frequent 'switch-offs' where my mind would be thinking about an impending situation in one of the companies. In many of my photos from family events and time with the kids, I would have one hand over my ear, clutching a phone, talking about work.

The coming-home-from-work boundary didn't exist as my electronic leash kept me tied to the daily ups and downs of the founders I supported. The VC business forces you to become a ruminator. Unlike operators, who go back the next day and attack a problem, we have to think about problems in steps. Is it enough of a problem? Are we focused on a less material item than something else that is critical? In what time frame do we bring this problem up as a priority at a board level? How do we frame the problem, and finally, how do we convince the founder to take it up and consider solving it?

So a problem has to be sliced, diced, analysed and prioritized before it can be exorcised! That is a lot of thinking. Unfortunately, I had not trained my brain to shut down the thinking process after I came back home. Over the years, these switch-offs would take a toll on my relationships and precious moments. Photos of me holding a phone would continue to accumulate.

The internal feedback within our firm from the previous year had pointed out that as directors, we should be the first port of call for our founders. Sitting in my office that day, I had found a strong mission in life through that goal. If I could be the director that founders decided to call in their hour of need, then not only did I help build a stronger company for our fund, but also helped build personal bonds with people we had embarked on long journeys with.

It was a period of exploration. Understanding themes and markets. Estimating the time to the future. A future in which mobile Internet was yet to be defined.

One day, in the fall of 2008, I headed off to south Delhi to meet the founder of a physical bookshop with a lean inventory model. The founder had set up small storefronts in cafes and hospitals. The idea was to understand the potential of taking the offline bookstore and converting the model to an online bookstore. Books lent themselves well to online sales with their well-established cataloguing system and favourable weight-to-volume ratio. I met the founder in his small office near Siri Fort. It was a nice sunny day, reminiscent of the Delhi winter days before the pollution went out of control. We both belonged to Dehradun, where his mother ran a bookshop. As a young boy growing up in Dehradun, I used to rummage through their discount section for Alfred Hitchcock mystery novels. The smell of musty paper was intoxicating. The older editions would be priced at less than ten rupees, and if I was lucky enough to find a new title, I would gleefully dish out the cash to add it to my collection.

The discussion on going online with the books business was free-flowing, and over cups of coffee, we both realized that the greater element involved in building an online bookstore was not intimacy with the book business, but a technology DNA in the business. On the way back, I stopped at IIT Delhi to catch up on the progress of a start-up that was building a search tool using SMS. Six SMSs was what it took to find the name of the movie playing in the local movie theatre. In the open area, which served instant coffee and Maggi noodles, the founder and I talked about how people in India would access online information. People were motivated to access critical information, no matter the pain. Would people use clunky methods like SMS to search the web because there was no other way?

We also closely evaluated a business that foresaw a world where people would carry two separate devices—one for voice and one for email and web. The founders felt that telecom companies had tried unsuccessfully to integrate the two and the world needed to go back to a consumer portable device that was tailor-made for the Internet. Our internal thinking was stuck on a basic problem—wouldn't it be a pain to manage two devices? Thank God for simple doubts.

As investors, we were excited by the quality of founders, but we were reworking the nature of business models that would work in India. India's domestic markets had grown and as a VC firm focused on India, we saw the on-ground increase in the demands of a growing economy. The frustrating part was that the role of technology in building scale businesses seemed to be limited. VCs in India were beginning to fund playschools, agri-trading firms and eye clinics. We were in a services economy and the concept of a 'product' was not clear. We were a generation that saw IT service companies develop process frameworks that well-trained people delivered. Indian companies could manage accounts of a US 500 corporation from an office in Gurgaon. Insurance claims could be reviewed by a company in Chennai. There was confidence that we could put together services and deliver them consistently. If we could do it for US customers, we could do it for Indian consumers. But where were the founders who could build technology products?

As a team, we shared a belief in investing in non-capital-intensive businesses and businesses that relied on India's service delivery capability instead of manufacturing ability. Given a choice, we would have restricted our focus on moving bits, not atoms.

Why was capital efficiency such an important criterion? No one had seen a VC-funded business valuation get anywhere near a billion dollars and no one could imagine any Indian start-up hitting that milestone. If you can't sell for a lot, you don't build companies by using a lot of capital. So capital efficiency won high marks in our deal selection. Building a large workforce was not a challenge in India. We chose to focus on education, financial services and retail services as our key markets.

Our annual strategy meeting for the year concluded on an upbeat note. We were seeing exciting service companies addressing long-term structural problems in India while remaining capital-efficient.

4

Every VC fund has three years to deploy its capital. The investments that the fund makes and its overlap with the big companies that are born in that three-year window will determine the success of that fund. A VC friend of mine described the investment period in a half-serious but not entirely inaccurate manner. Funds invest in three phases— the first part of this three-year period is when the team has fresh capital: newly raised, ready to deploy. This phase is the 'clueless' phase where the investment team is making random calls. The second phase is the 'sane' phase where some semblance of structure is brought back and bets are usually more sensible. The last phase is the 'lazy' phase where the fund is about to run out and a new fund is being raised. The team is busy working on raising the new fund and some half-baked decisions are made without the usual zeal and diligence. There could be surprises, but the most likely winners, predictably, come from the 'sane' phase.

We started investing our $210 million second fund in 2008. It was deployed in two bursts—a few new investments in 2008–09 and then more actively in 2011.

Prior to the 2008 economic crisis, the world had witnessed excessive liquidity. Two hedge funds had invested gobs of capital in a company called Webaroo. The Webaroo team worked out of the SINE incubator inside the IIT Bombay campus. SINE was the earliest university-linked venture programme in India. Funded by government grants, the incubator is housed in a 10,000 square feet building in the middle of the IIT Bombay campus. An economically priced workspace in the city of Mumbai and access to student resources was its contribution to companies like Webaroo.

While SINE did not produce too many successful start-ups, it had a long-lasting impact on influencing future founders from the IIT Bombay campus.

Webaroo had been co-founded by two IIT Bombay grads who were based in Silicon Valley—Rakesh Mathur, who had previously co-founded Junglee (acquired by Amazon), and Beerud Sheth, who had co-founded Elance. Webaroo was working on building a browser for mobile devices. It had a team of highly qualified engineers who had set a high bar for independent product thinking and innovation.

The culture in Webaroo was engineering-driven and the team was allowed to tinker with ideas. One of the projects that the team had worked on was a product called SMSGupshup. This product allowed group messaging using SMS. SMS used to cost consumers about Rs 1 in 2008. Users could join interest groups and send and receive content on SMS for free. Value-added-service-meets-Facebook is how one could describe it. If WhatsApp had been around then, it would have looked like WhatsApp on SMS. The only challenge was that SMSGupshup lacked a revenue model.

I met Rakesh and Beerud in the Bay Area at an Indian restaurant over lunch to figure out what was going on in the business. Rakesh arrived in his Porsche. He was the quintessential Silicon Valley old hand. He knew his way around start-ups, raising capital and selling companies. Between dipping naan into American-made chicken curry, we talked about the excitement around SMSGupshup. Millions of people were already using the service to access content. Indian users were discovering and creating groups based on mutual interests and contributing content several times a day.

Many of the groups were for 'time-pass', like jokes and cricket, but some groups were using the service for discussions, news and opinions.

There was even a group for a nearly extinct north-eastern language that its members were trying to revive.

This was happening when Twitter and Facebook were in their early days.

I next met Devdutt Yellurkar, who was a partner at a VC firm called Charles River Ventures. We met on an unusually warm, sunny morning in a café in Palo Alto, located on California Avenue. California Avenue is the quieter cousin of the increasingly crowded University Avenue, which ends inside the Stanford campus. Its cafes do not face the high pressure of

University Avenue and carry a far more relaxed air. Devdutt lived close by and I always enjoyed meeting him.

Devdutt had founded a product business called Yantra and had run it for ten years before moving to the investment side. He was seasoned, with an affable personality that was a solid combination of Indian sensibilities blended with Western mental models. Devdutt had left India more than twenty years back but stayed in regular touch. We jointly evaluated several businesses in India, including the early version of Snapdeal. Devdutt and I synched up on Webaroo and its potential. He shared his thoughts in his usual straightforward manner. He felt the growth was solid. At scale, we can find ways to build a revenue model, he said, but Beerud should be located in India and not the US.

I came back sufficiently excited about the potential of backing a network that aggregated millions of Indian phone users. Was this a killer app for Indian consumers? Coming back to India, I shared my findings with my partner Ashish. We both felt that the future was not so clearly visible in this case— there was no revenue model in sight—but the outcome could be large. India lacked any form of online community, and while Google's Orkut had been most successful, the relative ease of being socially connected on the phone allowed millions of phone users from diverse backgrounds to come together.

My partner and I visited the SINE office in Mumbai to meet the team and understand the product in greater depth. The engineering go-to person in SMSGupshup was Venky. He explained to us the architecture needed to support a system where millions of users could read and contribute messages across carriers. The cost of millions of SMSs was borne by SMSGupshup. The team looked solid and Venky's thoughts on scaling the platform gave us sufficient comfort. The engineering team had members who were unknown then, but were learning the ropes well. Some of them would be starting off on their own in a few years.

Ashish and I finished our meeting with the Webaroo team and stood chatting at the entrance of the building that housed SINE. Tall trees shaded us from the Mumbai heat and curious crows stared down at us. The campus air was young and expectant. Students walked around in slippers and professors scurried around with a little more urgency.

Ashish and I could have discussions on any topic, from metaphysics to wine and start-ups to our kids. He would always start conversations asking about the well-being of everyone in the family. We both had moved to India from the Bay Area. We understood the venture business principally the same way, having seen it up close in Silicon Valley.

Ashish liked to have his views challenged, and discussions with him were always a learning exercise because he kept it simple but was earnest in his desire to understand the opposing point of view.

Standing under the coconut trees, we had one of our many future-gazing exercises. Here was a company that was taking a bold new step towards creating a massive platform. Its growth was natural. People seemed to like the experience and users contributed to and enhanced its value. The team was solid. We leaned towards recommending the investment to our partnership. The previous investment in Webaroo at a rich valuation had to be dealt with. With our partnership on board, Helion invested in Webaroo. Charles River Ventures also committed capital and Devdutt joined the board on their behalf. This would be his maiden venture investment.

The action at Helion continued. In the same year, my partners backed an eye-care chain called EyeQ. Healthcare delivery was a large, untapped opportunity. Specialized clinics in the areas of IVF, renal care, dental care, ophthalmology and even trichology were being seen as scalable opportunities. The valuations for investments in healthcare clinics had been set at unjustified levels because of a few investments that had just happened at rich multiples. Early-stage businesses were being valued at twenty to thirty times their turnover.

Scaling a clinic required getting qualified medical professionals and well-suited locations. Not unlike hospitals, the ideal teams were a combination of a medical doctor and a business head. The trouble with clinics was that much like restaurants, they had to replicate their success multiple times in order to reach the magic number of Rs 100 crore in turnover. This was fraught with risk and uncertainty. Scaling to 100 locations was already a tough ask. So one location generating a turnover of Rs 1 crore was considered a minimum expectation to keep the goal of multiplying to within reasonable limits.

VCs found clinics to be a palatable unit to fund. Each clinic had its own risk associated with location and functioning. The sunk cost was manageable. Unlike a hospital that would take hundreds of crores to build and carry a single-location risk, clinics could add up to the same revenue in a gradual manner without blowing through a pile of cash.

Prior to EyeQ, we came across a childbirth clinic that was attempting to make childbirth a pleasant experience for the expectant mother. The team was a combination of an obstetrician and a businessperson from a real estate background. A single location of a childbirth clinic could generate Rs 2-3 crore and lowered the complexity bar for the number of locations. This made it very attractive.

We decided to invest in this company and called a few VCs to co-invest with us. One of them liked the company so much that they decided to keep us out and funded the company entirely on their own. It was a strange experience, but we admired the VC firm for their single-mindedness.

EyeQ's co-founders were Dr Ajay Sharma, an ophthalmologist, and Rajat Goel, who had worked for an eye equipment business. EyeQ's mission was to bring quality eye care to the masses. They were focused on north Indian markets. They followed a model of setting up clinics from scratch and buying existing practices from eye doctors who were planning to exit. EyeQ could use this lever to add revenue fast. It also had a per location turnover in excess of Rs 1.5 crore, allowing for fewer locations needed to cross Rs 100 crore in revenue. We co-invested in EyeQ with Nexus Venture Partners.

2008 was a busy year at Helion. We invested in eight new companies. A beauty salon chain. A corporate long-stay using a network of apartments. A yellow pages company going digital. An ad network for online videos. A social network on SMS. A

B2B media company. A gift card company for offline retailers. The last one was a solar power company.

We ran into Inderpreet Wadhwa, who used to work as a software engineer at Oracle in Redwood City. He had quit, moved back and was trying to put together a solar plan in Punjab. India had an installed power capacity of 145 GW in 2008. Three-quarters of this was supplied by coal and thermal. Less than 10 per cent was from renewable energy and only .032 per cent came from solar! India faced a 12 per cent power deficit.

Inderpreet's company, Azure, had just won a contract to set up a 1 MW solar plant in Punjab. Inderpreet was a savvy entrepreneur. He had taught himself the intricacies of the solar business, and unlike most others who dabbled for the sake of quick flips, he had a long-term plan to build a power company.

His conversations with investors had generated interest from a Silicon Valley VC firm called Foundation. Foundation allocated a quarter of their latest $750 million fund to investments in clean tech. Silicon Valley had taken a fancy to clean tech and a few funds like Foundation and DFJ had doubled down on the theme. The business would not have made any sense to invest in for a VC other than at the time of creation. As it progressed, each project that it won would have to have its own balance sheet. It would ultimately own a string of pearls, each generating a long-term yield backed by government contracts.

It was now 2010. Getit was now a two-year-old investment. The organization had been redesigned to reflect the new structure. Our board meetings had fallen into a rhythm. We would meet every thirty or forty-five days to review the progress and in the interim help the founder work through issues. I would sit through interviews for the new leadership team and chalk out the organization's structure and lines of control multiple times with Sidharth.

A reasonably decent group of people had joined the company in finance, sales and technology. The CEO, Sidharth, was working on putting together the modern building blocks of the business. Data was the key to selling more and to a better customer experience when they searched for local businesses. Better data was the first area of focus. Cash was running out fast and running the legacy business was a drain on time and money. It would have been better off killed, but then it was still contributing to 90 per cent of the revenue and sustaining the large sales force. New leadership was taking time to become productive. The business still seemed to be more a group of parts than a sum of parts. What was causing this? The answers were not easy to find. Time had begun to run out and we had not even launched the new voice-based search service.

Culture and DNA are the hardest to change. Expecting a twenty-year-old organization like Getit to start galloping was a mistake. I overestimated the power of venture investment. The older an organization gets, the more set it becomes in its ways. Just like humans. A tech company's DNA is the most valuable piece of a start-up. This DNA allows a puny start-up to take on the might of gigantic competitors. This DNA needs a crack team driven towards a common goal with urgency. It produces exceptional products that deliver value to its users and immense growth, milestone after milestone. This DNA is the prerequisite to success in the VC business.

5

Life moves in circles. I had started my career working for the Securities and Exchange Board of India. As a young management trainee in the apex regulatory body for financial markets, I had had a chance to get a bird's eye view of the financial markets in India right from the regulator's early days. At my first job as a VC, in Walden, I worked with my boss, Somshankar Das, to invest in a payment company called Venture Infotek. With this unique background, I picked the straw for leading Helion's investments in financial services.

With the help of my associate and interns, we started to scope out the market. Our study led us to focus on two areas—businesses that distribute financial products and those that can create and distribute specialized credit products. In all high-growth economies, financial services are at the heart of consumption and manufacturing.

The majority of India's population was not even exposed to basic banking services. Banks were designed for customers who could leave a reasonable sum of money in their accounts. Bank branches would have kilometre-long queues if they opened their doors to the hundreds of millions whose incomes were small and went from positive to zero once a day. The banking system was not designed to serve everyone.

Microfinance companies had sprouted across the length and breadth of the country. Companies like Janalakshmi, SKS and Spandana provided loans to customers who could not be served by banks. In most cases, needy customers would otherwise end up at a local moneylender's and get caught in a vicious cycle of predatory rates. Microfinance companies would lend Rs 5000 for twelve months and this would allow the borrowers to tide over financial emergencies. These companies filled the gap between banks and moneylenders but in the process undertook humungous effort to lend and collect Rs 5000 from millions of borrowers while keeping it all cost-effective.

South India had a more well-developed credit culture and it was no surprise that the strongest of such companies had chosen to grow first in states like Andhra Pradesh and Tamil Nadu. Microfinance was a business at the intersection of social impact and responsible lending. Many of the founders came from not-for-profit backgrounds and had started their businesses purely for social impact.

Grameen Bank was started in Bangladesh by Dr Yunus and it had been successful in building a framework for social lending and joint credit responsibility. All microfinance companies followed the Grameen model of lending. Women showed tighter social bonds and tended to borrow and spend responsibly. They would seldom borrow for their own consumption—the purpose was usually to improve the living conditions of the family or generate income that would supplement the household income. The Grameen model required women borrowers to form social groups of five to seven. Loans would be given to each woman in the group but a collective responsibility was ascribed to the group. The borrowers tended to show higher responsibility for their repayments if their actions affected others in their social group. The borrowing group was socially tied together with bonds that acted as moral pressure points. No one wanted to let the other borrowers down. These groups were not restricted to villages.

Impact funds like Lok Capital and Caspian had made it their mission to drive financial inclusion by investing in microfinance institutions (MFIs). Regular VCs like us were seeing the potential of large businesses if scaled well—companies addressing a genuine need that was felt by hundreds of millions of Indians.

I started seeking out these companies and word got around quickly. We were invited to look into many of the start-ups in this space, and our cheque-writing ability also opened doors to conversations with the more scaled-up MFIs.

Microfinance was built in the fields by foot soldiers who handled lending and collections. Operational strength was their key to scale and success. My colleagues and I visited the lending centres of various microfinance companies to study their field operations. These visits took us to districts in Andhra Pradesh, housing pockets of blue-collar workers living in low-income areas of large cities like Chennai and the back streets of Jaipur. A centre manager would typically take care of ten to fifteen centres of the company. Each centre would be a meeting point for ten to twenty groups once or twice a fortnight. And each group had five to six women. We visited one such centre on the outskirts of Jaipur. We walked in the narrow lanes, jumping over open drains, through a world that played out in the open rather than inside closed rooms. Women were drying papads and knitting foot mats, and children were playing dangerously close to fast-moving traffic. We VCs in our neatly ironed khakis were discovering a new world.

The visit took us to a small house with a front room that could accommodate ten to fifteen people. Slippers carpeted the entrance while women sat inside on the floor with their group. They had come to make the weekly repayment on their loans.

We sat around and observed. The meeting was conducted by the centre manager, Vibhor Singh. With a formal beginning and an end, the meeting used rituals like recitation of oaths to establish group norms. The attendance of its borrowers ensured the discipline of a weekly repayment and the physical exchange of cash required a physical presence which kept the social contact live. The 'product' was not the loan. It was this meeting—customers walking in every week for twenty-five weeks, registering their participation.

The meeting started with a pledge to respect and uphold the relationship between the group and the microfinance lender. Collections were made in cash, accounts were settled, passbooks were updated and another weekly cycle passed. The group behaviour led to incredibly prompt repayments and losses rarely crossed 1 per cent.

This was a group of borrowers with no formal income, no history of formal credit and no credit score. They needed this loan so badly that they made sure their track record was impeccable.

The engagement was high and this ensured that the customer's intention to repay was not confused with inability to repay. The system self-adjusted because the group acted as a backup. I asked some of the women about what they did with the loan and how they planned to repay it. In that blue limestone-coloured room, the slanted rays of the late-afternoon sun streamed on to the weathered and anaemic faces of the customers. Voices eager to share life's aspirations chimed in, 'Our husband has no financial discipline so we are forced to play the role of the emergency fund', 'Taking a loan puts the onus on the housewife', 'My husband listens to me a lot more and supports my small business', 'I can pay for my children's school admission and make sure they get educated', 'I can buy more daal for my papad orders', 'I can buy waste plastic yarn to make more mats.' There were so many different voices in the room but every woman felt responsible for another.

The customers chatted around for a bit and then headed home to cook the evening meal for their families. The carpet of chappals reduced in size and then no more were left. The field manager walked us back to our car. He would cover many such centres and conduct these meetings every other day, collecting cash and filling passbooks wherever he went. He had grown up in a village close by and knew the terrain well. Multiply Vibhor Singh and his group of 100 borrowers 5000 times, and you can imagine the scale at which some of these microfinance companies were running. Five thousand Vibhor Singhs zipping around on their bikes carrying cash and loan papers for processing. People and processes taking credit to where it didn't exist.

We left Jaipur, slightly more convinced about the opportunity and tremendously lighter in the heart. The venture business had its memorable moments.

Mona Kachhwaha is a Citibanker-turned-impact investor. She was my neighbour in Dehradun. She was also the first investor in Equitas, a microfinance company based in Chennai. My quest for an investment candidate in microfinance brought me to Mona. We had not connected since we were in the eleventh grade. She now occupied an office in the same business centre where Helion had started—just down the road from our new office. Mona and I caught up on the past and were equally struck by how our paths had crossed again. I laid out my reasons for seeking her out. Mona, in her characteristic thoughtful manner and with the patience of a monk, walked me through the intricate industry structure of microfinance— the customer's need, the role of the banks, the players, and why all was not well with the growth surge in the industry. At the end of the meeting, I was clear that Equitas had all the makings of a large, sustainable company. A balanced head, a strong commercial sense and credibility was needed from the CEO to build a successful business. We had no doubt about the market potential after our Jaipur visit.

Mona put me in touch with Vasu, the founder of Equitas, and wished me luck. Investors had already started lining up outside Vasu's door. Mona and I met on a Thursday. On Monday, my colleague Nats and I were on a flight to Chennai to meet Vasu. Nats was flying in from Bangalore and I took the first flight from Delhi. We both landed within thirty minutes of each other and left the airport together in our taxi.

Before we reached Equitas' office, Nats and I had to make an important stop. Nats knew Chennai well so I let him guide us to the best idli shop in town. He was feeling quite at home. The office crowd milled around. Idlis light and fluffy as cotton wool dunked in coconut chutney and sambar. Vadas with a specific degree of fermentation, crispy brown from the outside and soft from the inside, came next. We scooped up the last dregs of sambar with the crispy side. After a satisfactory cup of filter coffee to round it all off, we asked our taxi to take us to Temple Tower Building on Anna Salai Road.

Temple Tower was a large office complex whose fourth floor housed Equitas' head office. It had a liftman who would press the floor buttons. We had to tell him the floor we had to get to. Surrounded by the smell of mogra flowers, we were lifted up to our destination.

Vasu met us in the boardroom. It was at the end of the hall, with employees busy monitoring operations and reports flashing on a TV screen. To the right of the hall were the executive offices, where we stopped to say hello to Bhaskar, Vasu's ex-colleague from Cholamandalam Finance. Vasu's room was right at the back, guarded by a super-efficient assistant.

The assistant guided us to the meeting room and we were soon savouring the day's second round of filter coffee. The assistant fired up the projector and a presentation titled 'Investor Meeting' popped up on the screen. This was a company which knew that investor meetings are not one-off events.

Before starting Equitas, Vasu had run the vehicle finance business at a large Chennai-based financial services company called Cholamandalam Finance. The team had followed him from the previous company and the organization structure had a well-defined map of the leadership hierarchy.

Vasu joined us in a few minutes. He was dressed in subdued formals. He sat at the chair that had the laptop hooked to the projector with his investor deck at the ready.

We introduced ourselves as an investment firm that had been set up on the principle of founders first. We described our recent investments. Nats had also been in the lending business at Wipro Finance and shared some of his past experience trying to collect capital from borrowers. We wanted to establish a connect and invest our time in building a relationship. The introduction from Mona helped us get off on a good wicket. He saw us as an investor that understood the social side of microfinance, but also intriguing enough as a well-known tech investor to add to his list of shareholders.

When the preliminaries were safely concluded, Vasu took over with an assured air of having real achievements. He began by telling us the story of how he thought about starting Equitas while on a visit to Stanford University. He came across the Grameen model of lending and was intrigued by it.

Vasu said very matter-of-factly, 'Equitas' mission is not very complicated—it is to be able to issue a simple loan of Rs 5000 and collect it on time. That's all. That alone would be enough to make this into a vast business.'

I was bowled over by this clarity. No fancy vision or missionary gobbledygook about uplifting lives or eradicating the scourge of moneylenders.

He then fired up the presentation and walked us in detail through the business and the way it was run. Sustainable growth was Vasu's credo. His confidence in his team's execution capability was very visible. His board was carefully chosen. His team was carefully chosen. His business was very profitable but he didn't gloat over it. Return on equity is a standard measure for lending businesses. How many rupees of net profits can be derived for every rupee of shareholder capital? In Equitas' case, the percentage was in the late twenties. For his sense of the natural order of balance, this was unsustainable because market forces would soon beat it down. He instead talked about how he would try to sustain it at 20 per cent.

Some of his management practices were unique, but they ensured the involvement of every employee. One of them was an all-hands-on-deck meeting where everyone got together in

Chennai for two days, sat on the floor of a hired space, ate simple meals with the leadership team and got a chance to talk about local challenges and best practices. There was a deliberate effort to tie the leadership vision right down to the centre manager.

Vasu's selflessness was an example to the management team. His salary was established as a fixed multiple of the lowest-paid employee. His ownership was already much lower than most founder-CEOs due to dilution from raising capital in previous rounds, but his vision of creating a large company was not tied to his holding.

Nats and I were surreptitiously exchanging glances. Vasu ranked heads and shoulders above most CEOs we typically came across. The company was more advanced than our usual stage of investment, but then, it had a long, long runway for future growth.

Vasu told us that there was an opportunity to buy out some of the early shareholders and we should let them know if we were interested. It was a meaningful ownership. This was beginning to get real.

We had done a top-down dive into microfinance, understood the market, determined which the most promising company was, and now we had an opportunity to buy our way into its capital structure. Nats was excited about the opportunity, 'It's a good one, man'. We had already had an informal call with the independent board member that Nats knew. 'I know about a lot of people on the team and they are all solid,' Nats continued. I was thinking about our lack of control as small minority shareholders.

I said, 'We may not get our standard rights', and 'We have never done an investment where we are not the lead investors.' We were still debating our next steps on how to move quickly on this investment when our flights were announced.

In our partnership meeting, we set expectations for our colleagues. Our protocol was to get the founders to pitch to the entire investment team in our office once before we finalized. Everyone shared their thoughts and any major objections were addressed.

Answers were provided for questions raised. The investment team also shared their individual views on the founders. This was to give collective feedback to the lead team. But the lead team had to be supported, ideally by the entire investment team or at least a majority of it. Much like the solemnizing of a marriage, anyone not supporting the reunion had to raise their voice or make peace forever. This process ensured that the entire team was behind the investment and took collective ownership of the group decision. Our partnership was designed to provide collective strength to our portfolio. Not only the investment team but even the extended team of operating partners was positioned to support the CEOs in achieving their goals. We had already seen some classic flameouts from our portfolio. There was no blame game directed at the individual who made the investment; the effort was to ensure that we did not repeat our mistake.

So the act of collective affirmation was important to ensure that the new investment was brought in as a new addition to the family.

With Equitas, we had to make an exception to our process. Vasu would not be coming to Gurgaon to present to the partnership. We would have to go to the fourth floor of Temple Terrace to hear him out instead! The investment team sensed our comfort in recommending a new investment in a new space. My fantastic bunch of partners were game to make the trip. If it didn't work out, at least we would all get to eat the best idlis money could buy!

Thankfully, the Chennai trip was about more than eating idlis. Vasu's vision came through in our partnership meeting. It was possible to imagine the business scaling. The execution was impressive. This time, we also visited the Equitas back office in an adjoining building, which served as a processing centre for all the loans. We came back and unanimously decided to invest $5 million in Equitas based on Vasu's guidance. Nats sent over formal documents to put a ring on it. Documents were signed and now, as per VC norms, we were formally engaged.

6

The 2011 IPL had kicked off. I was in Mumbai's Brabourne Stadium watching Mumbai Indians play Kings XI Punjab. A bunch of VC friends had decided to come out to watch the match. Sachin got out early and it ended up becoming a venue to exchange work notes with casual reverts to the match. The match ended and I left the stadium feeling good about the fun evening.

It was noisy walking out with the crowd but I heard my phone ring. It was Vasu calling from Chennai. Short call. Another fund had come in and for some unknown reason Vasu had decided to work with them instead of us. The noise in the background was not that loud suddenly. I could hear every word and slowly process it. How was this possible? We had signed a deal. This was unheard of. Who could it be? And most importantly, what would we do now?

The fun evening had suddenly been replaced by hectic calling. I called Nats first. What the hell was going on, man.

No idea. We have signed papers. Screw the signed papers, let's get our ass to Chennai ASAP. With a new itinerary, I headed to Chennai next morning with a mission to fight and recover our now dissipating opportunity to invest in the most exciting microfinance company in the country. Nats and I skipped the idlis this time. We headed straight to Temple Terrace. The liftman was still there. This time, we just pressed the buttons ourselves and the liftman gave us an understanding glance.

Seated in the boardroom once again, we were trying hard to keep calm. Why had Vasu thrown this grenade at us? Vasu came in calmly, smiling. We gave him a moment to repeat what had happened and then promptly unleashed our shock and disappointment. Vasu was registering something new. Investors are actually disappointed if they cannot close on what they have decided to invest in. He was thinking of this as casual; we would just move on to the next shiny thing. But our ferocity of disappointment caught him by surprise. We were not willing to give up. Vasu, we have taken approvals from the partnership. Vasu, we have done so much to get here. Most of our reasons sounded shallow. The real reason was that we had an understanding. We had a commitment. And Vasu got that. We bid our goodbyes with a hopeful 'let me see what I can do' from Vasu.

After a few days of an excruciating wait, we got a call from Vasu. We can offer you not as many shares as before but about $2.5 million. Same price, same terms. We will take it, Vasu. Disappointed that it's not as many shares as we had budgeted for, but we will take it. And we will keep adding to our shareholding at every opportunity.

So Equitas became part of the Helion portfolio. Who said good things come easy?

The Equitas investment provoked new thinking in the partnership. We were witnessing a market story that we had not come across earlier. Could we find more such companies that could have solid market demand and raise late-stage capital on fundamentals? Buoyed by this confidence, we made a move on another microfinance company called Spandana, which concentrated on the demand for credit in rural markets. It was a harder market to crack than Equitas, but Spandana had come up from the grassroots and its culture of tight operations had helped it scale.

We were referred to Spandana by our friends at an impact firm called Lok Capital. Vishal Mehta was the partner in charge of the Spandana investment for Lok. Vishal had worked at Capital One in the US before returning to India and co-founding Lok. He had exchanged his suit for a Nehru jacket and embraced the cause of impact investing. Discussions with him were refreshing in their honesty and intensity. In his permanent beard and professorial thick-framed glasses, Vishal would effortlessly marry the sociology of the country we lived in with the grassroots economic challenges it faced.

Lok was an early investor in Spandana and had guided its thinking on financial inclusion. Vishal was deeply engaged with the business. He introduced me to Spandana's G. Padmaja

Reddy as a value-added investor she could use to help her scale the organization.

Hyderabad did not have too many start-ups, so it was a rare morning when I flew in for the meeting. The flight cruised into the Deccan plateau and gently landed at the Rajiv Gandhi International Airport. Given the early hour of the flight from Delhi, I needed a strong coffee to awaken my brain as soon as I landed. Coffee downed, I was alert enough to understand all the nuances and complexities of a new company with more than a million customers.

The weather in Hyderabad was pleasant and a lovely blue sky welcomed us as we drove through the natural ramparts of grey granite on both sides.

A short ride on the elevated road from the Hyderabad airport landed us at Spandana's doorstep. The office was in a standalone building in the newly constructed commercial centre in Hyderabad called Gachibowli. Four floors and a basement housed the headquarters staff. A security check later, we were sitting across a large boardroom table from Padmaja Reddy. We were not alone—a posse of assistants was sitting around us, ready to intervene about any escalating issues.

Padmaja Reddy, the founder of Spandana, was a force of nature. Unlike many other founders we met, Padmaja was not someone with a long corporate career. Nor did she have a finance background. She had studied home science. But sitting in front of her, listening to her explain her business, one could mistake her for both those things.

Born in Guntur, Andhra Pradesh, Padmaja stumbled upon microlending after making a small loan to a ragpicker. She started her business as a not-for-profit and had already grown it to a reasonable size by the time the investors showed up. Always in a saree, Padmaja prided herself on supporting locally woven sarees. She was married and had a young son. She would start her day at 8 a.m. from home and end it at 2 a.m. in the office. She breathed life into the company every day. Padmaja controlled the massive network of field agents criss-crossing villages across Andhra Pradesh from her office. Her work was mostly done from the conference room on the third floor. Her leadership team dropped in and out through meetings.

Spandana had concentrated on providing loans to people based in the state of Andhra Pradesh (prior to the creation of Telangana) but appeared well-placed to scale across India. A focus on the rural population required a wider coverage of staff and offices. It was dealing with fraud in the field and overborrowing from customers who could not be verified, yet the company was delivering 99.5 per cent collections and making profits. Spandana ran their operations at a cost that was lower than that of all their competitors. Field staff was compensated with a variable component and was driven hard to achieve targets.

My main line of discussion with Padmaja was the organization. How did she plan to lower her span of control? Would she hire a CEO or COO to help her share the load? How far did she see herself leading the business?

Padmaja introduced her team, drew the organization chart on the whiteboard and detailed the products. The founder's imprint could be seen in every part. Considering there were so many moving parts, Spandana did not have too many supervisors—perhaps that was the reason for its low cost of operations.

Jeff Bezos, Jack Ma, Steve Jobs all had their life energy injected into the companies they built and ran. They were often larger than life and under the spotlight all the time. The risk could be a single point of failure, but if they scaled, these founders could steer their creations through good and bad times—the latter often being periods where professional leaders fail to resurrect failing start-ups. Over the years of investing in start-ups, our own thinking about founders had evolved. We had come across founders who would not scale and a high-potential company would start going sideways.

The obvious idea of replacing the founder would be brought up. In most cases, it would be a difficult conversation. Founders would begin politely, putting it off to 'when the time is right'. Most would say, 'We ourselves would like someone who is better suited to run the organization', but when the time came, they resisted fiercely. And even where a replacement was made, it rarely succeeded. Despite the competency and the compensation, the replacement of a founder by a professional could not be accompanied by the life energy that only a founder can provide to a start-up. So a founder's ability was also measured by the life force they could provide to grow an organization.

Padmaja had demonstrated scale in all aspects of growth. Spandana had reached a scale where scores of banks lent them hundreds of crores of rupees every year. The balance sheet was built on a small equity base—the company had raised capital sparingly. This was a risk for lenders but generated high return for equity holders. Spandana was generating solid profits. I met the leadership team and understood their priorities. One common question I asked everyone was 'What do you worry about most?' Concentration of business in one state was the common answer. What was brewing in the market? I knew that two other microfinance companies, Basix and Share, had been competing with Spandana for the same customer. Surveys had pointed to overborrowing in certain districts around coastal Andhra Pradesh. There was also a third angle—the state itself was active in providing loans to the underprivileged and microfinance's 'success' in reaching millions of customers was considered to be the 'evil machination of capitalist goals'. Most constituencies, especially the ones with greater leaning towards social goals than capitalist goals, did not appreciate the cost efficiencies that size could bring—in the growth stages of any sector, large companies have to take most of the market share. Like any sector, microfinance had to generate leaders too. Many participants in the space did not agree with the belief that growth leads to better governance and cost efficiencies for the customer.

Armed with financial spreadsheets, interview notes and updates on a new round of investment that was under discussion with a south-eastern private equity fund, 'ABC PE', I went back to base.

For a few days, our analyst had been crunching away at the Excel sheet that modelled the business in numbers. He had applied scenarios of a bad year hitting the company, which set growth backwards, and also assumed some pressure on the return on equity as the company raised more equity.

Armed with the worksheets, we both sat down in our conference room with the Excel sheets projecting on the big screen and our lunches growing cold. The white screen reflected the numbers from the overhead projector. Row after row of assumptions, presenting a detailed picture of how each year was expected to unfold. What were the most important drivers? What could go wrong? The business was lending and collecting to consumers who were woefully short on credit in a market that was larger than what Indian lenders had ever witnessed. We couldn't assume a doomsday scenario. Let's lower the leverage in the business—reduce the debt they can take and only increase if they have more equity—yeah, sounds like a reasonable scenario. Business grows from fantastic to great. Not a problem. Still very investment-worthy. Let's increase staff cost for the field force with additional spending on training and throw in more supervisory staff. Oh, the cost has gone up, but still plenty of room to go. Damn! Whichever way you beat them down, the business still looked attractive. What about growth rate? When does the business slow down? With the current products, another five years before we came even close to market over-penetration.

We decided to take a break for lunch. We slowly chewed the morsels, now cold and dry, rolling around the complex dependencies in our heads with our mouths full. Sips of Diet Coke helped us swallow the food.

What is the worst-case scenario looking like to you? Probably something dramatic. Something in customer behaviour caught our attention. I stopped chewing.

All it needed was a large enough group of customers who refused to pay back the loans, and then the behaviour would spread like wildfire. We were familiar with something like this in the past. Customers were closely networked and a refusal from one pocket of customers to pay back had become a contagion for the industry. Wow—do you think it might repeat itself? After the last episode, Spandana and other lenders had become alert to such risks. We had specifically focused on this topic when we met the team in Hyderabad. But was a recurrence possible? Absolutely. Let's sleep over this and stress-test the model again before we recommend the investment to the partnership. With the jarring thought of the fragility of the business lingering in our heads, we adjourned for the day.

7

Next day at work, we were back in the conference room, staring at the bright light bouncing off the white screen. The doomsday scenario had been mathematically modelled as a large hole in the balance sheet, but one that did not spread the fire beyond a specific geographic region. The model passed this stress test. We then ran a pricing analysis. Were we paying the right price? Could we make returns that would meet a VC's return expectation? Did we see a minimum five times return from our investment? In what time period? The lunch was pushed back this time. Rather eat late than eat cold food.

So what is it? This was usually more a rhetorical question. For most of our businesses, a return calculation was so far out that by the time we had finished the exercise, we were convinced that our strongly imaginative minds had churned out yet another story. But it was a necessary exercise. Many 'promising' businesses had no chance in hell of giving us strong returns. Our diligent analyst did his best to bake in the reality and the expectation to arrive at a 'reasonable' estimate. Spandana was a '5x'. And it was an easy one to exit. We also had a defined role to play. Padmaja liked our backgrounds and was excited to work with us. ABC PE was negotiating with Padmaja to invest a large chunk of capital.

'This is a big bet,' I told my partnership. We were looking at an amount greater than $5–10 million and at a valuation we rarely saw. 'We have got to believe in the long growth cycle ahead. It can give us at least 5x from here.' This was 2010 and scale companies were not appearing every day. Here was a prime example of growth and execution. And most importantly, a company that would have a high 'exitability' score. Exitability was now an internal measure of how we saw the chances of an investment going public or being purchased by another investor. Wider demand to buy out so we can return capital to our investors. We needed this score because we realized that factoring this in at the time of investment helped us see the journey ahead better. The partnership gave the go-ahead for the investment and we were back in Hyderabad, sitting across from Padmaja. Around the boardroom table, the crowd had increased. The acting CFO, a banker from Mumbai and an existing investor visiting to discuss the ABC PE investment were all present. We all sat around the table exchanging business cards and listening to Padmaja's conversations with everyone. The energy at that table was palpable. There was a discussion on the size of the ABC PE round. Padmaja wanted to sell some of her shares in the round to realize a small liquidity but the existing investor was opposed to the idea. The banker was there to water the relationship plant. One day, it may flower into an opportunity to manage the IPO. Discussions half done, Padmaja ordered biryani for everyone, and soon the banker, the investor, the CFO and us were joyfully shovelling down spoonfuls of the fragrant rice. We returned to Delhi excited about our new investment.

The unpredictability of life is often forgotten. Most of us are blissfully dismissive of it till a rude reminder wakes us. Most of the time, it appears that we have a good handle on how events unfold around us, with mild interjections of surprises. But the exothermic reaction we call life is far more unpredictable and chaotic than our minds would allow us to imagine. The VC business is a microscopic view into this cosmos of continuously flipping coins—of not only the sudden unfolding of chaos but also the bounce-back of ships believed lost in storms. You go to bed feeling good about an investment and you wake up to a shitstorm. You almost conclude that an investment is not going to break through, and just before you turn the lights off, you hear the jet engines revving. How do we undergo this and still keep our sanity?

The ABC PE investment hit a wall. The existing investors felt it was not necessary to raise the round and dilute themselves. There were many conditions in the round that were unacceptable to Padmaja and to us. One of them was to allow Padmaja to sell some of her shares. Investors controlled strategic investments through rights that they bargained at the time of investment. Sometimes, every investor has the ability to throw a spanner into a highly contentious investment—a founder is caught between a new investor and the existing investor, who has the right to say, 'No, I will not approve this new round.' These rights are called affirmative rights and can make a founder's life very hard.

Not having a fresh slug of $100 million from ABC PE meant that Spandana would have to continue to grow its loan book by borrowing new capital from banks on an already stretched balance sheet. I was sitting in the playground with my son when I got the message about ABC PE. He was on the swings, asking me to push him higher. I tried to concentrate on remaining in the moment, but after some pushes, I said screw it, and dialled Padmaja's phone. Moving out of shouting range of my son, I opened optimistically, 'Hey, hi, Padmaja how are you? I just heard there is a challenge in closing the new investment. Where are we on ABC PE?'

'The ABC PE name was very strong and they were also giving good terms, Rahul.'

Was? Were? My mind registered these two words more than others.

'I am not sure how we can revive this deal. It's not going ahead. They have formally pulled out. The $100 million would have given us a lot of strength with our borrowing.' Padmaja sounded very frustrated.

I got off the phone and noticed a mild headache. My thoughts were drifting to the worst-case scenario of our analysis. A strong balance sheet is the best defence against credit losses. My thoughts dissipated as my son, done with his playtime, came over and asked to be taken home.

The shitstorm was brewing.

It was only March in Delhi, and like every year, conversations would invariably start with the topic of 'how hot it had become'. The temperature at home was high also because the kids were on vacation and had to be kept engaged throughout the day. They were still young. The younger one had turned six and the older one was nine. The heat would be a serious deterrent to stepping outside the house. Showers were not helpful as the water in the pipes was gurgling at 70 degrees. After a full day of all three of them driving each other nuts, my wife would eagerly anticipate my return from office. She wanted her sanity back. I had attempted making wood-apple juice at home because I heard that it acted like a coolant for the body and mind. The kids hated the taste so I had to finish most of it. Iced tea was their favourite but the caffeine in it made matters worse.

One day, I got a mail from my friend Mona introducing me to a team of ex-bankers who had left their well-paying jobs to start a micro-housing-finance business called Shubham.

Sanjay Chaturvedi and Ajay Oak had come together to start the retail finance business for Reliance after a long career in banking. I was intrigued but did not follow up. It was a paper plan and there was too much going on between Equitas and Spandana. But the team stayed in touch. They intended to focus on the enormous problem of housing for the large population of Indians who were self-employed and needed mortgages to fund their home purchases. The duo had settled on solving a problem that had eluded the largest mortgage finance companies in India as it involved figuring out the creditworthiness of a customer class that has neither predictable income nor credit history. Our own study of the opportunity had started only recently and we were still in the process of building our understanding.

One of the obvious challenges was the lack of affordable housing in India. It seemed like a chicken-and-egg problem. If there were not enough low-cost homes, what were customers going to buy? Ajay and I had a few common friends besides Mona and I would often hear about them. To understand this situation better, we called someone from the top leadership of HDFC, the largest mortgage finance company in India. What we heard confirmed two important elements—HDFC felt that affordable housing was a mega opportunity, and despite their might, they felt constrained from entering. It needed a new approach which their existing infrastructure would not support.

Sanjay and Ajay would drop in periodically to update me on their plan. Sanjay was senior to Ajay at Reliance and Ajay maintained the arrangement in the start-up as well. With his father in the Air Force, Sanjay had grown up on Air Force bases. He had a jovial personality and had done his time running credit businesses for multinational banks. Ajay shared Sanjay's relaxed air and always had a disarming smile. Ajay had started his career at ANZ Grindlays and ran the mortgage business for Citibank in south India. He had the business down cold and used his Citibank training to think entrepreneurially. Ajay had the reassuring personality of a wicketkeeper and was a safe pair of hands who would never drop a catch. Unlike the other founders, who had some element of personal zing, Sanjay and Ajay were just regular, hard-working, good guys.

The two got along well with each other, and with their complementary skills, they made for a strong pair of founders.

Both had young families, and throwing away big pay cheques had been a tough but deliberate decision. They unabashedly joked about relying on their wives' incomes to run their households.

Coming from the sophistication of Citibank and HSBC, how would the duo work things out in the grime and filth of unauthorized housing colonies, which were not even on the radars of the city municipalities?

In one of their visits, they talked to me about an area of Delhi that most of us would not even have driven through after living our entire lives in the city. Savda Ghevra was one such outpost that they spent time studying. It was a resettlement colony in which uprooted slum dwellers were allotted 18 square yards. This was a pressing case for affordable housing. Spread over 250 acres, the colony had about 8500 such plots. At Rs 15 lakh apiece, the total housing loans needed to build homes in Savda Ghevra alone added up to Rs 1275 crore. This opportunity was for one of fifty-five such resettlement colonies only in Delhi.

The question that was waiting to be solved was, how did one go about assessing the creditworthiness of borrowers using new means of underwriting? Shubham had picked a massive gap in India's housing market, but how would it go about executing on it?

Sanjay and Ajay had to have not only the chops to build a mortgage business but also address the unique needs of a customer class that had some very distinct challenges. Both founders had given up their suits for half-sleeved shirts and jeans and had started meeting people to understand their lifestyles and income patterns. Sitting in the home of your customer is the best way to design your product. The insight that came from these meetings was key to determining the approach. The customers had no real assets, so a home ownership would be their first step towards financial well-being. Households that own homes move progressively towards better financial stability. Household incomes were a combination of two or three members in the family pooling together their pay cheques. Many more customers already owned homes and needed money to add a room or restrooms or better roofs. So, in addition to new home purchases, a second product was conceived for home improvement.

Another focus market on the outskirts of Delhi was Mangolpuri. It was an old settlement that had undergone a full transformation from barren plots of land to thousands of families living in houses with clear title deeds, besides hospitals, schools and government amenities. Shubham's first branch was expected to come up in this neighbourhood. Ajay and I took a car ride to this market to help me understand the business. Some opportunities are so early that you have to walk in the founder's shoes to understand them. Ajay and I had a good chat along the way. I discovered that he was a state-level badminton player but had given up due to knee trouble. His parents still lived in Pune, where he grew up. His wife worked at Citibank in the area of risk management. He had worked all over the country. The Reliance Retail job was based in Mumbai, for which he would travel from Delhi every week. Sanjay and he met at Reliance and built up a bond spending long hours flying back and forth to and from Mumbai. On one of these flights, 'the meaning of life question' had struck them and they found patient listeners in each other.

After an hour's drive on the highway to cover the 30 km between the haves and the have-nots, our taxi turned into an area with the familiar blue municipality signs. We were still in Delhi . . . but not really. This was what a large mass of blue-collar workers called home. It was hard to imagine what this place would have looked like twenty years back. Perhaps like what Savda Ghevra looked now. The street layout seemed planned. Our walk started from a government school. Single-row houses ran side to side as far as the eye could see. Some were in their original form and some had disproportionate extensions dangling from here and there. Rooms jutted out uneasily. Gnarly metal staircases connected the old parts with the new. Extensions in families seemed to mirror the extensions in houses. Jagged boundaries made it hard to ascertain where one house ended and the other began.

Most of the families Ajay and I met had jobs in Delhi or small production units for goods as diverse as apparel, dentures and plastic moulding. Many families were the original plot owners from the time that the colony had been carved out. The extensions were being paid for from monthly savings.

Some bricks and cement would be bought on day one, and the unfinished structure could then stand for six months, awaiting more funds. A single project could last a whole year. Many interviews later, Ajay and I headed back to what we thought was 'Delhi'. Where consumers like us lived. Mangolpuri had been a revelation in more ways than one. I learnt about home ownership—it came piecemeal for these families, but with affordability more widespread than I imagined. The inventory already existed.

My concern about the market was the lack of new inventory. New affordable housing had to be built to fund first-time buyers. This was dependent on builders focusing on this segment. Research did not indicate a surge in new homes coming to the market. Given its inevitability, we parked this concern. The business model was also driven by loans for home improvement and we had seen evidence for that in our market surveys.

We backed Sanjay and Ajay with a small investment to begin with. Housing finance required a licence and Shubham had not gotten one so far.

Sanjay and Ajay prepared a plan that would maximize the capital that would be lent out for new loans. This meant we had very little left over for overheads, including founder salaries and office space. Sanjay and Ajay proposed a salary for themselves which was more like a token than a pay cheque.

Founder salaries are Gandhian tools to keep the balance between founders and investors. They are Gandhian because it's a moral position achieved through a personal sacrifice. How much is a founder's salary worth? When everyone around the table knows the salary-earning potential of a founder who has chosen to take an income only for sustenance, the power of that moral stand helps maintain the balance in the board.

As an investor, I have tremendous respect for founders who forego high salaries to put the company's interests first. The cash is limited; it can be dissipated in high salaries or be used to build more equity value for everyone.

I saw an example of this in Mr Ashok Soota, co-founder of IT services company Mindtree. After the dotcom collapse in a tough market, he decided to cut his salary in half. As a young VC working at Walden, I was awestruck by this act of leadership by Ashok. The board had to work hard to convince him to consider a cut that was not too deep! Avoiding self-gratification has a direct impact on the leadership culture in organizations.

Two modest offices of Shubham were opened—the 'headquarters' in Gurgaon and a branch office in Mangolpuri. The headquarters was inside a shopping mall with thin footfall. Showrooms selling construction tiles and bathtubs occupied the rest of the floor. To help get the new business off the ground, I started spending a lot of time with Sanjay and Ajay. Being the 'local' VC in Gurgaon naturally helped. I enjoyed the sessions and began to appreciate the opportunity even more than when we had decided to invest. Our sessions, punctuated by nicotine breaks, were to discuss the scope and timing of the launch of the business. The idea was to go ahead full steam without delays once we obtained the licence.

The customers were concentrated in pockets like Mangolpuri and needed a local branch to walk into. So the branch office in Mangolpuri was a model that would be replicated in every market. We wanted each branch office to have a short payback period because we knew that we would need many such offices and we had to be as capital efficient as possible.

The credit process was conceived as a combination of personal interviews with customers and assessing the financial information on the paper application. All businesses need to have unique intellectual property (IP) in order to compete. Underwriting a formal loan for a customer with an informal income was Shubham's key value proposition. Between the branch office staff, the central credit team and the customer, a new loan application process had to be set up. The sourcing team had to get a feedback loop to guide them to understanding customer backgrounds. The sourcing team interviewed the customer—how did this convert into a decision? Shubham had to build this differentiation.

Shubham became a licensed housing finance company six months after we filed our application. Helion and Elevar invested the balance capital, and the business was launched.

The staff at the branch office, who had been scoping the market, now started informing residents that they could take loans to purchase houses. These customers would not be considered by other lenders, not because they had a bad credit history but because they needed a new evaluation method.

After some fits and starts, the Shubham train started moving and quickly picked up speed. Within three months, the company had opened a second branch office in Ghaziabad in Uttar Pradesh. We were finding that in these markets, home improvement loans were not in as much demand as we had estimated. They were complicated to monitor in practice. So a major assumption in the business was already disproved. To our surprise, there was enough turnover in the existing homes to drive demand for home purchases. So we were not as dependent on new homes being built as we thought we were. At this stage, every new loan we gave was a cause for celebration.

Over the next three years, Shubham expanded to twelve states and eighty branches. The slow, complex unfolding of a company started: from a paper plan to an intricate form—employing people, training them, raising capital, balancing growth and risk.

Between Equitas, Spandana and Shubham, I discovered an India that had been alien to me. It was all around me but I had never paid attention. I only saw what was familiar. I noticed problems that affected people like myself. But here was the largest mass of India—desirous of asset ownership, toiling for upward mobility and a better life, and yet unserved. This quiet but large opportunity was hidden from many investors. Someday, a VC could do very well marrying technology-led business models with this opportunity.

8

We were in the beginning of 2010. Four years had passed since we wrote our first cheque from our first fund.

Our portfolio had grown to twenty-five companies and covered a wide range of technology-led and non-tech consumer businesses. We had almost fully invested our second fund. All of us were leading peripatetic lives, meeting new companies and visiting our investments. The routine had me catching daybreak flights into Bangalore and Mumbai three to four times a month. The new airport in Delhi was inaugurated in 2010 and the 4 km length of the airport made sure I got my walking exercise done first thing in the morning, especially when the flight gate was in the fifties.

The air travel industry had also grown, with several new airlines catering to the low-cost domestic traveller. The average Indian had started to try out the wonders of air travel. The speed and convenience of flying across cities was unbeatable. India's domestic air traffic had grown to 60 million passengers, with sixty-seven planes taking off every hour, but the industry was suffering from intense competition and crippling fuel prices. The losses for Kingfisher Airlines had intensified.

The intense competition was beneficial for the OTAs (online travel agencies), which took the lion's share of ticket sales. MakeMyTrip booked 1.6 million air tickets in 2010. When we had invested in 2006, the annual run rate was 36,000. Deep had done a fantastic job building the business, successfully competing with two other OTAs to retain market leadership. The company had raised more capital. The private capital arm of a global hedge fund called Tiger had joined as an investor. The new headquarters now occupied more than 15,000 square feet.

Technology still remained the weak link. Hiring for the top role had been hard and all the investors were assisting in the search. The quest for quality talent had taken us far and wide to Indian and foreign shores. Some of the hires did not work out and some good hires left too soon. This had left the technology function on a weak wicket.

The battle for mindshare made the marketing function equally important, and also the recipient of the largest allocation of money. TV campaigns, creatives and newspaper ads were adding to the cost of customer acquisition. The marriage of offline media with online businesses was beginning to happen for the first time and marketing heads were still deciding whether they should advertise for more transactions or to build a brand. In the process, investor capital was being burnt with very little to show for it.

In 2006, Naukri produced the iconic 'Hari Sadu' campaign—a smart mix of wicked humour and a key message had given the commercial high recall value. Sanjeev Bikhchandani, who founded Naukri.com, had a background in advertising. He was also on the MakeMyTrip board. Deep continued to use his board effectively for the areas he needed help in. The marketing function was formalized and new leadership was brought in from consumer companies.

MakeMyTrip started spending more effectively on marketing. Transactions grew and the brand established itself.

MakeMyTrip worked on its IPO all through 2010. Rajesh Magow, co-founder and CFO at that time, architected a successful IPO on Nasdaq. The stock price 'popped' 70 per cent on opening and provided handsome gains to investors who participated in the initial stock offering. We offered some of our shares in the IPO and returned the capital to our investors. MakeMyTrip started being traded as MMYT on Nasdaq, making it the nineteenth Indian company whose ADRs (American depository receipts) were listed on an American exchange.

UnitedLex, the legal services company, also picked up traction, with seventy-five US clients now signed up. While the initial set of services was for legal contracts and IP, the foray into helping US corporate clients with their litigation costs turned out to be the best fit with market demand. Canaan Partners, a US VC firm, joined us in the next round of financing. Alok Mittal joined me on the board as Canaan's representative. Just as the Canaan round was finalized, the profitability of the business began to show itself. The company became so capital-efficient that it barely needed to use the cash raised in this round.

The company hired a COO in Gurgaon with a solid track record of managing outsourced business processing operations. Despite this hire, the challenge of 'process-ifying legal work' was not easy. Lawyers were not ideally suited to deliver on process frameworks. UnitedLex had moved out from the business centre into a 13,000 square feet space in the DLF SEZ in Gurgaon. We were worried about utilization of this magnitude of space, but the growth surprised us. 'We need more space. We need to hire more people' was a common board meeting declaration. The CEO, Dan, based in Florida, had an insane travel schedule. But the absence of an India-based CEO was deprioritizing the culture focus. A large group of intelligent people working without clearly defined cultural expectations was not healthy. This was a people business and client requirements were intense. Confidentiality, credibility and very little room for error. Like all enterprise companies, the scale-up required building up a sales team—people hired from outside who could replicate the founder's style of missionary selling and also convert it into a coin-operated machine.

Among the many interesting growth hacks that Dan had used to build the business, a unique one was how he could bring on board a group of high performers who had a proven track record of growing client revenue. The expertise that came together as a group was indispensable for a services business. Dave Deppe and his colleagues had joined UnitedLex and brought with them a deep domain expertise of selling and delivery of highly sophisticated litigation-related work to large US enterprises. Deppe and team were based in Overland Park, Kansas. Sitting close to hectares of farmland, Overland Park was also famous for being the headquarters for Sprint Corporation, the fourth-largest telecom operator in the US. The Sprint headquarters were built on plots meant for seventeen buildings, occupying 4 million square feet of commercial real estate. From 2009, Sprint had started subletting their world class facilities to other companies. UnitedLex took space in one of the Sprint buildings and thus Overland Park became the location for UnitedLex's corporate headquarters.

We had a board meeting in Kansas City in May 2011. We caught a United Airlines flight from New York to Overland Park. Getting off a narrow-bodied jet, the first thing I noticed at the airport were signs for tornado shelters. The wide-open expanse of the Great Plains gave ample room to tornadoes. The new UnitedLex office was impressive—orderly and well-equipped. The rental was lower than that of their Gurgaon office space!

We had a detailed business review with the leadership, which had become very US-centric by then. Each business head was mapped to a delivery head who could be in the US or in India.

UnitedLex had tried many variations of selling to customers. So far, the failure rate of a regular salesperson was guaranteed. We did not have the luxury of an IT services company because our buyer expected to be sold a concept and the only person who could give them enough comfort to make them finalize a contract was a domain expert in law. Despite these open questions, revenues had doubled every year. In 2010, Pangea3, another legal services company, had been acquired by Thomson Reuters for $100 million. UnitedLex's growth had resulted in PE investors calling us with a desire to invest or acquire the company. It was too early to consider a sale.

Back in India, an exciting start-up called RedBus had launched a service to sell bus tickets online. It had slowly and painstakingly gone about bringing together offline bus ticket inventory from bus operators across India. The other part of its business was an online consumer-facing ticket booking site. Unlike MakeMyTrip, which could access the ticket reservation system that agents were already using, RedBus needed to first build the online reservation system. Bus ownership was micro-fragmented and needed patient stitching together. The patchwork of inventory started coming together on RedBus' reservation system. Phanindra Sama and Charan Padmaraju were batchmates at BITS, Pilani, which is also my alma mater. They had joined BITS in 1998, taken up electronics engineering and landed similar jobs in Bangalore. Phanindra was the more outward-facing of the two. We had come across each other in one of the BITS Pilani events where Phanindra (better known as Phani) was also presenting. I liked this very thoughtful, self-aware founder immediately.

Even with no fundraise plans in mind, Phani and I would spend time understanding the business and talking about the challenges he was facing. We developed a good rapport and kept exchanging notes.

My partner Ashish and I would visit the RedBus office in Domlur in Bangalore and meet the team. The sparse office, located in a small lane, stood well-hidden from the hustle of the Old Airport Road and the swank of the luxurious Leela Hotel. We loved the frugality. The business was a brick-by-brick build-out—it required slow adoption by bus operators. It was a difficult business to build at first, but its defence moats were raised higher every time a new bus was added to the network.

We were sure the market demand would increase but didn't know when. RedBus had kept their cash burn very tight. Their capital needs were kept at minimal levels. This would ensure that they would not be out of cash when they needed it the most.

Phani and I stayed in touch but not as regularly as I would have liked to. Mumbai-based Seed Fund had already provided the seed capital to the company. Now, as Phani started raising the second round, we missed the bus because our attention was diverted somewhere else. By the time we got around to it, a lead investor had already been decided. Our relationship with the founder had been strong but our timing was not. We felt frustrated at missing the opportunity to invest as a lead investor despite knowing the company intimately.

We were investing out of a $210 million fund so we had to have a minimum cheque to write per company, otherwise we would have ended up with small ownerships in more companies than we could manage. Our investments had to generate at least $50 million to move the needle on returns on the fund. So when we were offered a tiny cheque in the round, we were hesitant at first. We knew that the size of the round was small and the company should raise another round soon. We would have an edge if we decided to lead that round and in the process we would have deployed enough capital, which would also give us a shot at generating meaningful returns for the fund. We became investors in RedBus in 2011.

Over the past two years we had also invested in several non-tech consumer services businesses like the beauty salon YLG, clinics like EyeQ and Dentys and quick-service restaurants like Mast Kalandar Restaurant and Brand Calculus. Our firm was designed to be a tech investment firm. But the openness to explore new opportunities was also part of the DNA.

We had a broad thesis on the verticals we would look to invest in—healthcare, retail services, financial services and education. Each of these verticals had to be dived into. We had to come up with an investment thesis for each vertical.

The spectrum of consumer businesses was wide and we had a diverse mix of companies in the portfolio. These businesses were very different from each other. We were not the only VCs to build a non-tech portfolio, but every firm had their unique learning from these investments. Many of them were obvious. A people-intensive business meant that any learnings were slow to provide feedback into the business. It took quarters before fixes became assimilated into the business. Selling a service to cost-conscious Indians meant the business was being squeezed at both ends: pricing made sure that margins remained under pressure and input costs kept creeping up. In financial terms, the operating leverage was low. Units like a store or a clinic took time to become profitable and until then losses accumulated. Every VC was focused on making sure that their own investments survived. Very little cross-firm investment happened for non-tech services businesses.

Most investments were slowly plodding along. But like all good investors, we were making sure we consumed these services ourselves. So our default office food orders were from Mast Kalandar. We could choose from a variety of north Indian food as long as it was vegetarian. The Mast Kalandar founders wanted to build a restaurant brand that served only vegetarian food. Affordable, high-quality food in neat packaging—this was the value proposition to the thousands of young, single, homesick north Indian IT workers who missed 'home food'. Both founders came from IT backgrounds and had never run a food business before. After the Helion investment, the founders started adding to the management team.

YLG had made a splash in the Bangalore market and become a recognizable brand. It was a beauty salon that catered solely to women. Brand Calculus had the Indian franchise for a Canadian brand of smoothies called Booster Juice. Its founder was based in Canada and had been a co-founder of an apparel brand in the late nineties. Each of these companies were dependent on commercial physical space. Real estate prices determined store feasibility. As most of them realized sooner or later, customers weren't really spending enough to justify store costs. High-quality commercial real estate in most metros is scarce. For a start-up to be dependent on such an expensive input to 'test its thesis' is self-limiting.

Store design had to be minimalized to reach break-even. Trained staff was churning out faster than they got hired. YLG even set up its own training institute for beauticians.

In offline businesses like restaurants and clinics, the hardest part is figuring out scale because their growth is linear. Variability never goes away and there are always plenty of variables that can stall growth. Would a new location work out? Would customers eat more at the store or would only new stores cause growth? Of course, there have been brands like Dominos, Starbucks and McDonald's that have defied these notions. They had access to food tech, which made their supply chain more predictable and customer experience more repeatable. Linearly growing businesses that are not VC-funded have to fund their growth from their own profits. The founders are forced to figure out profitability early. Being VC-funded removes this very important constraint of being economically viable at every step. So VC-funded linearly growing businesses have to overcome two challenges. First, they have to figure out the economics after they have established unprofitable practices. Second, they have to raise rounds of capital from investors who would always be wary of growth slowing down.

Technology-led businesses tend to scale better because they grow non-linearly and they are rewarded early when they prove this. Their growth is called the 'J-curve': there is a point in the journey where the original thesis is proven, the unit metric works out and then pumping in growth capital causes a nearly 90-degree curve upwards, taking the business to the stratosphere. At least that's the principle investors have in mind. The business starts getting rewarded with a premium valuation because there is a clear expectation for growth.

So here we were. We had more than dipped our toes investing in non-tech services businesses. There were hardly any large, existing brands in these areas. It was a 'wide open space'. It provided an opportunity for rapid creation of household brands in India with predictable, quality services. Would we be successful in creating large enough outcomes for our fund with this thesis? There were naysayers who believed that it was hard enough as it is—on top of that, lack of differentiation in these businesses could further hurt the chances of these companies attaining rich valuations. As with all things VC, we had to try it before we knew how it would play out.

9

My family and I had moved from Palo Alto, California, which was home to Stanford University, the melting pot of the top tech talent from around the world. We had opted to introduce our kids to middle-class India and let them grow up appreciating the opportunities they were getting versus feeling entitled to them. We rented a home in Vasant Kunj in south Delhi. The values of middle-class India had also evolved since I was young. It was foolish to assume that in a consumerist society made up of aspirational parents who themselves had grown up being deprived due to economic constraints, denial would be considered a parental value. Entitlement was being fed all around us.

I was being an idiot trying to create a make-believe world from the 1980s for my children. Added to this doubt, after two years of sitting in traffic jams, I realized I could put the time I spent in my commute to better use. Moving closer to work would mean shifting to Gurgaon. A mosaic of villages and high-rise condominiums, Gurgaon had a mixed reputation at that time, especially for south Delhi residents.

Gurgaon was considered to be a 'down-market', back of beyond location to live, but in the wild hope for quiet evenings with family instead of sitting in traffic jams, we moved again. This was another change, hopefully for the better.

At work, the next business we funded was a company operating rural schools. The founder was an ex-management consultant. We were biased about founders who had previously worked as consultants. Would they theorize more than execute? So, in order to assess this, we dived deep into the execution skills of this founder. The school was designed for students who lived in semi-urban belts around large cities. Their families aspired for them to learn English and computer programming. The government-run schools in these communities lacked teachers. A low-cost school that could replicate itself through better teacher training could grow into a Rs 100 crore business. The business had been planned for rapid scaling by using standard processes that could be replicated. Like a McDonald's. Cut, copy, paste. We had been looking to invest in a school because we felt that the market opportunity was huge. Here was the package of market and model. In reality, the scale-up was far more challenging. Just putting together the first school was a taxing journey. A day-by-day journey of discovery. And unlike a McDonald's, a school needs time to mature, for systems to settle down, for practices to be adopted.

Sometimes a pre-existing thesis leads us to invest because we like to confirm our own conclusions. But the thesis is a theoretical construct. A start-up that fits with theory is just a source of comfort that we look for. In the VC business, it is important to be aware of a 'thesis confirmation' bias.

Meanwhile, the political climate around microfinance had been tense in the past few days and with Spandana's Rs 1000 crore exposure in Andhra Pradesh, I was trying to keep on top of developments. Excessive gloating over the successful IPO of a microfinance company called 'SKS' caused a stark contrast between the condition of the borrower and the 'lenders'.

There had been fifty reported suicides by microfinance customers in Andhra Pradesh.[1] The total number of customers for microfinance was close to 5 million in the state. The political backlash had put the spotlight on the aggressive practices followed by microfinance companies. Frequent update calls with Padmaja were revealing the complex interplay between state-level political party agendas amid the conditions that were giving microfinance companies a bad rep.

On 15 October 2010, I was hosting some close friends at home. We had known each other since eighth grade and it had been a fun evening. I had a barbeque going in the front lawn and I was in charge. There was nice wine to go with the food and the weather in Gurgaon was perfect to sit outdoors. My friends were sitting around the barbeque.

Around 9.30 p.m., my BlackBerry started buzzing. I had been very careful about not burning the food on the barbeque but this buzzing somehow compelled me to pull out my phone.

I squinted to read in the dim outdoor light, and an email containing breaking news from Andhra Pradesh confirmed my worst fears. Now oblivious to the barbeque, the implications of what I was reading started to slowly sink in. The ongoing battle of words between the state administration and the 'high-flying' microfinance companies had escalated to a full assault. The state had passed a promulgation that banned microfinance activity in the state. This promulgation would throw three of the largest microfinance companies under the bus. A total of Rs 7000 crore would go up in smoke.

We all had burnt food that night.

In the next few weeks, the complex network of operations that was helping collect 99 per cent of the loans from millions of customers was dismantled. Politicians told borrowers not to repay their loans. Microfinance company employees who went around to collect the loans were arrested. In all our modelling of possible risk for Spandana's business, we had not created a scenario for a fallout with a state government. We had evaluated all possible risks—all of them would have caused some losses at worst. An obliteration of half the balance sheet was not even a doomsday scenario. Which brings me back to Padmaja being a force of nature. Here was a founder who had risen from the grassroots and built a business large enough to consider doing a public listing. Her net worth if Spandana had listed then would have been a few hundred million dollars; not that she was exiting and pocketing the profit. In one night, Spandana had gone from a profitable high-growth company to a company with Rs 1000 crore to be paid back to its lenders.

A lesser founder would have given up at this stage. Most go two steps forward and one step back, but to fall from a height to near death takes a different mindset. Padmaja picked up the pieces. She and her team were back in the conference room, sitting around the long table, coordinating the resuscitation. So we had hope of a revival and the support of the Reserve Bank of India, which recognized the social importance of microfinance.

In the 2009–12 period, some companies stood out because of how close we came to investing in them. Not once but multiple times.

Yogi was a business we looked at thrice but did not invest in. Based in Gurgaon, this company sold tech support to US consumers. We were one of the first investors to be called for their first round. There was limited investor interest and we could have gotten a favourable deal.

The company was an interesting twist to our focus on investing in outsourcing—instead of selling to US enterprises, they were selling directly to US customers. We knew some of the team members from past lives. This time around, we passed it up deliberately. We were not convinced about the thesis and the delivery challenges from India. Canaan Partners, which had joined us in UnitedLex as Series B investors, invested $3 million in January 2007. The company grew well and we felt we had missed investing in it.

The second time they came out to raise capital, we did a full-blown deep dive into the business. The company was more or less on track. This time, though, we were one of many VCs looking. The company's profile had grown and we had to compete. This time we made our offer but fell short of the best offer. Not willing to pay up, we passed with some regret in our hearts. This round was led by Sapphire Ventures from the US in July 2008.

In 2010, the company came back once more, but we were more passive as the ideal stage for our entry had passed. We had some more regret about passing up the last round. Only if we had paid a few million more. Our woe worsened when we heard about their impending Nasdaq IPO filing. Over time, these feelings reduced in intensity, but the memory of the multiple shall-we-shall-we-nots remained fresh.

Another company we were drawn to multiple times but did not invest in was Canvera. Canvera, a digital photo company, was founded by Dheeraj Kacker and Peeyush Rai. The compelling personalities of the founders prompted us to return over and over again for a relook. The sheer tenacity and ability to pivot was inspiring to watch. It was the case of A-grade founders in a B-grade market. The market they pivoted into was the wedding photo album business. They installed sophisticated printers and used their past knowledge of printer technology to create photo albums with superior finish.

Since wedding photos were the domain of local photographers, the other part of their business was helping these photographers upgrade their wedding album business through Canvera's suite of printing products. It was a network business that needed adoption from both photographers and customers. Dheeraj was a CEO admired by many VCs but not many got over the hump on the business.

Vinay Sanghi had founded a company called CarTrade. He knew more about second-hand cars than anyone I knew. CarTrade was aggregating the second-hand car supply in India. This was a business I passed on twice! Invited to be a first-round investor, I again got caught up in the market size. I liked Vinay as a founder but the second-hand car market supply chain seemed too cartelized to mediate in. Vinay had run Mahindra's First Choice and knew the business inside and out. I was second-guessing him! Deservedly, Vinay went on to attract top-tier investors and built the largest platform for second-hand cars in India.

By 2011, the seeds of e-commerce in India, sown in 2008 and 2009, had begun to sprout. Compared to China's 150 million online shoppers (out of 450 million Internet users in 2010), India had an estimated 1 million online shoppers (out of 70 million Internet users). There were a few traditional players who offered e-commerce as an extension, like RediffMall and Indiatimes, and there were a few new e-commerce-only companies like Flipkart. Flipkart had added digital media to their large catalogue of books.

Tiger Global had invested $10 million in Flipkart in the summer of 2010, fuelling its growth. In 2010, Flipkart also introduced cash on delivery on their orders, and that helped it grow four times during that year. In 2011, they were expected to grow seven times. Tiger Global, which had so far invested in JustDial and MakeMyTrip, had shown a new path for e-commerce investing. A young business like Flipkart had been valued at a forward-looking valuation and this had perplexed the Indian VC ecosystem. The estimate for the capital needed to build a profitable business was eye-popping and no one knew of investors with so much capital.

We had only one evidence of a large capital infusion in Flipkart and were worried that the capital needed to build a horizontal e-commerce business was not available in India.

Our experience with JiGrahak still rankled. A business that loses cash to growth needs to have a lead investor who can afford to carry the company on their shoulders for a few years. There was a paucity of capital that could be deployed unless there was a visible light at the end of the tunnel. No one knew in 2010 that Flipkart would raise $5 billion. Even a fraction of that seemed highly unlikely.

The US experience of Amazon needing a never-ending supply of capital was justified by the gargantuan size of the American retail market. E-commerce was a 5 per cent subset of the total US retail spend of $3.8 trillion. In India, organized retail was less than $30 billion.

Indian consumers, especially the ones not living in metros, were frustrated with limited choices being carried by formal retail stores. Till they visited a metropolis like Mumbai, they had to delay their purchases for lack of choice. The demand for fashion and electronics were the largest. Brands like Samsung were also feeling constrained by lack of retail distribution.

Horizontal markets thrived on the breadth of their catalogues and inventory management. The purchase was efficient because you were in a supermarket and would find every possible type and variant of what you wanted. Becoming big was a prerequisite for success.

Vertical markets like Diaper.com and Zappos.com had created a unique customer experience. Customers knew where to go when it came to some of these products because the keyword was 'diapers' or 'shoes'. These keywords registered in their mind and were reinforced by the customer experience. Small but defensible castles could be built without the risk of depending on large rounds of capital.

Hence, keeping in mind a capital-constrained market and customer experience differentiation, we felt vertical businesses would be more attractive companies for us to fund. Our investment strategy leaned towards finding online businesses that targeted a narrow category of goods.

Once this was clear, we started scouting for businesses that were beginning to emerge on the e-commerce map. One of our associates came across a company called LetsBuy.

LetsBuy was the first online business in India to focus solely on consumer electronics. It had been founded and bootstrapped by Hitesh Dhingra in 2009. Hitesh had taken personal loans to get LetsBuy started and had carried the company on his shoulders. Operating out of a small office in Patel Nagar in central Delhi, the founder had carried forward his learning from running CafeGadget, an online store for gadgets. Hitesh had worked at Tyroo Media and his new business had two angel investors. Hitesh knew the category well and had deep relationships with brands like Microsoft and Samsung. An eternal optimist, Hitesh had a relaxed demeanour. His friend Amandeep was a supply chain consultant at Ernst & Young. He quit his promising job and joined as COO. Aman made a good tag team with Hitesh. He was oriented towards keeping track of financials and could identify cash sinkholes.

LetsBuy was a bootstrapped operation, but Hitesh's relationships with brands helped him bring on big consumer electronic brands early on. Many of these brands worked with twenty to twenty-five large-format retailers, but none of them had an online presence. Brands liked the idea that a direct-to-consumer operation could extend their sales channel. They were enthusiastic to support the business because Hitesh understood the back-end sourcing better than anyone else. What he lacked was technology muscle. Before we invested, I asked him what he could have done better in his previous job. He was honest enough to admit, 'I wish I had built a better tech team.' At LetsBuy, Hitesh's efforts were lacking in the same area. Not coming from a strong tech company background was a handicap for him in hiring top tech talent.

LetsBuy's reference calls revealed that they were beginning to be recognized by electronic brands as a dependable alternative to Rediff.com and Indiatimes.com. Mobile phones were less than a quarter of their sales. Laptops, digital cameras, pen drives, external storage and TVs were flying out of the door. Sales in metros and sales in Tier 2 cities were split in half.

Accel was also interested in the company but they had concerns about overlaps with their investment in Flipkart. Tiger, the other backer for Flipkart, was also interested. Accel felt that the business needed additional work to build out the front end.

In September 2010, we closed a financing with all three investors investing equal amounts. Given the thin team structure, we insisted on creating a larger than usual pool of shares to be used for hiring future employees.

With a solid round closed, Hitesh and Aman started to ramp up the business. This was my first time at an e-commerce business. Seeing it scale, I had a hard time appreciating the hyper growth. While growth is good, to me it seemed unplanned and led by market pull. It seemed crazy at first. Opening the front end would result in solid sales growth, but then the back end would come under pressure. The business needed a supersonic speed of execution to keep pace.

What was happening was like filling a tank with a leaky bucket. A business with operational issues, like a leaky bucket, loses more cash than it makes, but how does one discover the holes without filling it? This quandary had made the rapidly scaling business a dynamic mixture of grow, fix, repeat. Growth led to more cash outflow because most of the orders were paid for by customers using cash on delivery. Cash on delivery had become the dominant mode of payment since Flipkart had launched it the previous year. Courier companies would take a month to collect and bring cash from customers. Customers who returned goods that they ordered but never paid for were causing an even bigger dent in the cash balance. A large funding round was becoming imperative despite the vertical focus.

Board members Prashanth, from Accel, my colleague Ashish and I would meet in the LetsBuy office. Their new office was, incidentally, MakeMyTrip's old office in south Delhi. The same place I dreaded driving to during my early days in Delhi. MakeMyTrip had by now established itself as the leader in the online travel space and we had happy memories of that office. We joked that the MakeMyTrip success would rub off on LetsBuy.

Hitesh was confident that growing the top line would improve their chances of raising the next round of capital. Within six months of our round, we had grown our sales ten times. Diwali 2011 was coming and Hitesh felt that they could blow the numbers out of the water if they could fund it. Hitesh's optimism in raising a round was colouring the execution. How would we run an e-commerce business going at full speed with depleting cash in the bank? What was true for most businesses founded in this time frame—the occurrence of growth and near-death experiences—started being repeated more and more often.

We started talking to investors for the next round. The most solid option was a $42 million round put together by a syndicate of three VC firms in India. All of them had global affiliations and were people we knew well. The round would put together a formidable group of investors behind one company. We signed the term sheet and the investors forwarded $5 million as an advance investment. Diwali was a bumper season that year and LetsBuy sold as much as it could manage. The big sale also made a big hole in the cash balance. To complicate matters, one of the investors in the syndicate insisted that the company switch its structure. The process was lengthy and expensive but it had been proposed as a necessary condition for the balance funding. Top legal and tax consultants were brought in to advise the company. The paperwork was done, and after four months the new structure was in place.

These four months were crucial. A lot changed in this extended period. Instead of closing the $42 million round, the financing was stuck in the restructuring. The investor who insisted on the cumbersome restructuring backed out of the deal while agreeing not to ask to be returned their advance investment. The other two VCs in the syndicate stayed committed, but wanted a new investor to replace the one who exited. The syndicate was shaking and the round was crumbling. Now it was up to Hitesh to find a replacement.

The Diwali sale also forced the investors to take another look at the cash numbers. I was sitting in the Delhi office of one of the remaining VCs from the syndication of the three VCs. This VC was well aware of the damage a pullback like this could lead to. It was gratifying to hear the company's interests being put first. But reality is always brutal. 'The company needs not $42 million but $65 million in this round for Hitesh to execute without running into a cash crunch,' was his conclusion.

'But can't we go ahead and close what we have between Accel, Helion and the two of you?' I was pushing to somehow see the round materializing between the two new VCs. 'Besides the four of us, we need a new VC who is deep-pocketed and can write the big cheque when needed. None of us is that big,' was the answer I got. Raising $65million was a formidable task. With Tiger also being a lead investor in Flipkart, the conflict between the two companies had ruled them out as investors. With cash running out, Hitesh was meeting as many investors as he could and trying to stitch a round together.

Meanwhile, the Flipkart marriage option was being repeated with more regularity. Flipkart was doing well on its own but electronics was looking like the dominant category of the future. Buying LetsBuy would supplement their efforts and eliminate the possibility that a competitor would live on to bite at their heels. Better in than out.

Where we stood now—starting up, first round of funding, unbridled growth, a big round forming with marquee investors, a big round crumbling, talks of a strategic sale—it had all happened in fast forward. The pace was overwhelming. So far, I had seen that the founders' approach to building out the business had less to do with the market pull and more to do with what the internal constraints dictated. The company building process was more 'in control'. Teams and sales grew steadily. Cash was consumed at a predictable pace.

I would often tell founders, 'The market will happen, we have to stay ready for the big wave, and until then, let's build a great product.' The team would plan for longer terms and remain in preparation mode. Many founders would go to the other extreme and hesitate to spend capital, choosing to keep the company in the lower gears. Other than in microfinance, I had so far not heard that 'market demand is infinite so let's grow as much as we can'.

The LetsBuy experience was unique in two big ways. One was the approach of the founders to the market. Right from the scale of growth to the size of spend, there was no hesitation. There was conviction in the market opportunity and timing. The second was the market's acceptance that companies need to burn through tens of millions of dollars to build a business. This acceptance was new. It had been absent when JiGrahak was founded. Investors were on both sides of the table in the debate on whether this was right or wrong, but they all accepted that this was the only way to fund these transactional businesses. Indian VCs learning the formula for funding high-growth companies was a turning point in the history of venture capital in India.

Before the year ended, the decision was made. The round was still looking for the elusive third investor. Cash was running out. We decided to go with the Flipkart option. There was not enough cash runway to keep going as an independent entity. Flipkart bought out all our stakes in LetsBuy.

Flipkart was a good option—its own valuation was high, but it was growing fast. At that time, we just didn't know how fast. In reality, it was a lot more than we thought.

The brand did not survive within Flipkart but for a small price, Flipkart had eliminated a potential rival. The Flipkart value grew several times from that point onwards and we could exit our ownership in it with decent returns.

So, in the end, it turned out okay for us, although having a unicorn in LetsBuy would have been way cooler.

10

Ashish and I had our firstborns a year and a half apart from each other. Ashish and his wife, Nita, extensively researched which products were the safest and most suitable for their newborn. In the US, stores like Babies'R'Us carried a multitude of choices for every conceivable product for babies. It was overwhelming to make a choice. It was a mind-boggling experience for first-time parents to decide what was essential. When we had our first child, Ashish handed me a well-thumbed book written to help new parents learn about new brands and safety features—three-point harness versus five-point harness, for instance, or front-facing car seats versus back-facing car seats, cribs with drop-down sides with or without wheels, diaper disposal kits, humidifiers and so on.

It was immensely helpful. Considering India's baby boom, we felt that dynamics similar to the US would develop in India. It fit with our thesis to invest in vertical e-commerce opportunities.

In India, there were few baby product brands, and barring one national retail store chain, nothing existed that provided a wide shopping experience for parents. Most parents relied on the local chemist to carry a few items, and most clothes were hand-stitched. Mothers in India were just beginning to learn about 'maximum-absorption gel diapers' that guaranteed a full night's sleep for their babies!

A few start-ups had launched businesses in the baby care retail space. FirstCry and BabyOye were the prominent ones. We met the BabyOye team in Mumbai. They were located near Santa Cruz station in Mumbai with an all-in-one facility, just like LetsBuy's first office. Warehouse in the corner and the rest of the team floating around. Founded by a husband-and-wife team, BabyOye was one of those businesses that had been based on a need felt personally by the founders, who then went on to solve it. Like Phanindra Sama not being able to get bus tickets to go home for Diwali, the BabyOye founders also felt frustrated by the unavailability of baby items in traditional retail for their own child.

The other company we looked at was based in Bangalore. It was the coming together of a well-rounded team—a husband and wife who were already running a popular retail store selling baby items, paired with an early employee of Myntra. We liked the combination of category know-how paired with online retail experience.

Hoopos's logo was a purple octopus! The team cared a great deal about merchandise quality and customer feedback. We decided to invest in Hoopos as the sole investors. Accel and

Tiger funded BabyOye. Now we were competing with each other in an unproven category. We were betting on the category being deep. We expected that new parents, being Internet-savvy, would find it compelling to painlessly buy products for children. Growth in orders was slow to begin with, but we were convinced that it would pick up.

In early 2012, we seed-funded a business called TaxiforSure. It was founded in 2011, two years after Uber had tested its app-based cab ordering service in New York using only three cabs. In its early days of building a taxi aggregation business to serve customers in Bangalore, TaxiforSure was providing about 100 rides a day. The company was looking to scale up five times with the help of these new funds. The idea was to provide assured taxi bookings and a decent ride experience by creating a two-sided marketplace. The business was founded by two IIM Ahmedabad alums—Raghunandan and Aprameya—and was focusing all its energy on tight execution and customer experience. They followed a brute operational approach to aggregating a highly fragmented supply base, which had never been rated on customer service. Helion and Accel came together once again to fund this start-up, which was one of five similar start-ups, all at similar stages of evolution.

One of these five start-ups was Ola. Ola was executing aggressively and preparing for a market demand explosion a lot earlier than TaxiforSure. Ola was aggressive in its execution and spending substantially more on technology. Uber's popularity was limited to the Bay Area at this point. The first time I heard about Uber was from my friend Sundeep Peechu of Felicis

Ventures during one of my visits to the Bay Area. He could not stop talking about the tech-enabled experience of a taxi picking you up from where you stood and you stepping out at your destination, all without any cash transaction. Indian taxi aggregation start-ups were not yet designed to provide such an experience.

By the end of 2012, we had a portfolio of forty-four companies. The team at Helion had grown too. We had an investment team of seven investment professionals and two operating partners. These investments had taught us a lot.

Across the investment team, we had our own standards for assessing the quality of the founder-CEO. We needed common ground instead of going the way of the five blindfolded men touching the proverbial elephant.

So we conducted an exercise to study the strongest CEOs in our network. What made them tick. Why one CEO was more successful than the other over the long run. We arrived at a set of common attributes that these CEOs displayed. These attributes covered resilience, lack of greed, humility, action orientation, vision and strategic thinking. This framework was far from perfect, but it forced us to think like a team.

Our understanding of tech businesses had evolved with the fast-changing environment. We were using a team of analysts to help us keep track of new start-ups. Our goal was that at least 80 per cent of all start-ups operating in our sectors of interest should be talking to us about their next round of investment. This was an indicator that we were a preferred partner. If entrepreneurs did not want to talk to us, something was wrong. Our spectrum of investments had been broad, so we were seeing all kinds of deals.

After seven years of looking at Silicon Valley start-ups, when I moved to India, I used to struggle to size up a company in the Indian context. I would often compare Indian start-ups with those I saw in Palo Alto. I would therefore fail to factor in the context. One of my partners, Sanjeev, suggested I start building a fresh framework to evaluate Indian start-ups and stop comparing. I agreed completely.

I decided to observe as many companies as I could to construct the new framework to help me learn what I liked. In any given week, sitting attentively and actively responding to about ten to fifteen investor pitches was my run rate. I had been doing it for the past fourteen years. The trick to remaining focused while listening to so many pitches was to maintain a balance between volume and quality. I had not followed this rule. Now, after five years of this high-volume absorption, I was beginning to lose the joy of hearing new ideas. Was it because I was seeing the gap between high-octane pitches and on-ground reality? Was I getting more circumspect, or was I just plain jaded? Did I need to take a break?

My own theory about the reason for this exhaustion was that I had kept a broad focus for too long. Focusing on financial services had helped—I had been able to add unique value to my portfolio and I could also draw on the strong network I had developed in the financial services industry.

In 2012, I turned forty. I woke up feeling different. To celebrate our fortieth birthdays, three of my closest friends from college, who were also turning forty that year, decided to mark the events with a celebration of their choice. Someone did a Goa getaway. Another had a big get-together in Bangalore. I invited my three friends on a week-long 'boys' trip to the Ladakh region in north India. We visited monasteries, sat on hilltops without talking for hours, and caught up on chatting during the six to eight hours we spent laboriously covering distances through the lunar landscape every day. We all came back slightly transformed.

I thought more about mortality and how we made others feel. In an informal chat, I often heard founders talk about their meeting with VC A or VC B—they didn't talk about how smart the VCs were about their space. They didn't talk about how cool their offices looked. They talked about how they felt after the meeting. Did I have to take it upon myself to point out that the odds were stacked against them being successful? With so much variability in their lives, was one meeting at a given point in time enough to predict accurately their potential and how their businesses would do?

I was meeting many individuals who had chosen a difficult path. I had been losing the opportunity to understand their spirit. Here was a daily opportunity for me to revitalize myself. I just had to be more compassionate. The culture of a VC firm was on external display when its team interacted with its start-ups. This interaction was tricky. In most cases, we knew that we would not end up investing. The founders would pitch to us in earnest expectation. We felt that the least we could do in turn was to keep the session meaningful and engaging. The team had to do this without appearing dismissive or smug. We definitely didn't know the business better than the founder.

I started working on changing the nature of my exchange. I worked on establishing a human connect with the battle-worn founders—their stories, their triumphs and their epic fails. What did that lead to? Over time, I felt more connected to them.

Our team was split between our offices in Gurgaon and Bangalore. The culture in the team was beginning to stand out. We were the quintessential middle-class-background folks with very similar values in life. As a top VC firm in India, we were a desirable place to work. We were not the top salary-paying firm by far. Our main draw was our culture of encouraging participation and inclusion of all the team members in investment decisions.

We preferred candidates who reflected humility because we wanted our employees to treat start-ups with respect. At the same time, they had to be sharp enough to understand the complexities of a new business every week. If finding smarts and humility in the same person was not hard enough, we also had to look for another complex trait: long-term orientation.

Many people equate being a VC to a job that needs financial acumen because it involves investments. People new to the VC world do not appreciate the long-term implications of decisions. We had to live with our relationships and our decisions for seven to eight years. For us, financial returns were tied to the outcomes of our portfolio: when companies exited and we generated profits for our investors was when we deserved to be rewarded. So the unique aspect of our hiring process was looking for candidates who held a long-term view of businesses.

Our second VP hire was slightly controversial. We had been looking at candidates for a while. We got a call from a friend who was mentoring someone working at another VC firm in Bangalore. This person was looking for a change and wanted to talk to us. He dropped in and met Ashish at our Bangalore office. The VC world was small and hiring from this pool was not the best way to make friends. He reached out to us looking for a change. We were not poaching him from the other VC firm. Despite that, we were going to cause some bad blood with the firm where this person worked. The first meeting did make it clear that the candidate had well-thought-out reasons to look elsewhere.

I met him at the DLF Golf Club in Gurgaon. This was a regular venue for our team meetings—we loved the green golf course stretching all around us in the middle of the urban sprawl of Gurgaon. I too liked the candidate and after multiple meetings we ended up hiring this person. In the process, we burned some bridges.

Our firm's operating value-add was in two areas, finance and human resources (HR). We realized that start-ups lacked access to strategic HR advice from seasoned professionals. Most high-quality HR professionals were employed by large corporations and were unaffordable. Strategic HR became a perfect value-add to start-ups that were looking to scale. Our HR partner, Dhruv Prakash, was a seasoned professional. He did a great job applying his knowledge to the start-up environment. MakeMyTrip was building a leadership team. Start-up founders get so used to the informal and scrappy period of operating that the lack of a formal organization structure continues even during the scale-up phase. The task of deciding a formal structure seemed like a big challenge. Most founders would expend their energy in hiring the next-level team and assume that once you throw professionals into the pit, an organic structure would evolve effortlessly. This was where most scale-ups fail. The effort to integrate this team of hires was where the real effort was needed.

Our HR partner demonstrated this aspect of company building to our firm and to MakeMyTrip through an extended engagement. He took the entire team through a journey of defining a common vision and establishing a structure. This exercise had been a success in helping MakeMyTrip transition from a founder-run company to a leadership-driven organization, still headed by a founder. It helped them achieve a lot more without breaking down. This exercise became a template for us and we started applying it to many other companies in our portfolio.

By the end of 2012, our first round in the ring as a VC, which started in 2006, was coming to an end. The strength of the alchemic reaction between VC capital and entrepreneurial acumen was jumping up a notch. Big believers in technology had arrived on our shores and we could not live in a vacuum any more. The markets were no longer lumbering along at glacial speeds. Wild horses on energy drinks were pulling them forward. Capital was creating markets instead of creating companies.

Past lessons were ringing loud for both sides. The mistakes were now no longer hidden under the garb of slow markets. VCs and entrepreneurs had to up their game. Most VCs in India had taken after VCs in Silicon Valley. Two factors were likely to drive the recasting of VC firms going forward: billion was the new million and young unproven founders were now the norm. VC firms had to understand this change. They could no longer dip their toes with a few million dollars at stake. With the kind of capital needed to build companies now, VCs had to be 'all in'.

11

In the six years since we founded Helion, we had established ourselves as one of the most prominent VC firms in India. It's hard to determine exactly where a firm stands in the market, but it's easy to get a feel. Just ask five sought-after founders whom they would like to take capital from, and if four out of five put you in their top three options, then the firm is doing its job well. We were on the top-three lists of many founders in 2012. The top investors in the world had placed their trust in us. We stood for something. The market saw us as a trendsetter.

Our portfolio was now a broad mix of companies. Consumer Internet companies. Enterprise software companies. Beauty salons. Restaurants. Juice bars. Clinics. NBFCs. Many of these were clearly not using technology as a differentiator. There was no technology in the DNA of these start-ups.

Our default was investing in technology companies. I used to invest in optical backplanes in Silicon Valley, for God's sake. Non-tech investments had made sense for us, but only when they were opportunities in wide open spaces. The early-mover advantage was the single largest motivator. Lack of broad follow-on funding support took away this advantage. In financial services, the non-tech sector that I focused on, growth, and hence follow-on funding, was not a problem. Clinics, beauty salons and restaurants were not businesses we were likely to invest in over and over again. Now that tech was pervasive, we could switch back to our default view of the world—that tech would take over everything.

This transition to 'tech first' had to be done consciously as a firm. We had a strategy meeting in Bangalore. I landed in Bangalore from a US trip and headed straight for this internal meeting—we had picked a hotel in Whitefield for this off-site.

We were all seated in a small conference room with a white chart in front of us. My partner was going around the room, speaking on where each of us saw the world heading.

Not all of us saw the world shifting in the same way. There was a solid debate on which opportunities were still looking attractive in non-tech. There was an argument about why we had seen enough to support the fact that change from a 'consumer' to a 'consumer-tech' opportunity was now permanent. The question at hand was—do we as a firm go all in into technology investing or do we continue to straddle both tech and non-tech themes? Would founders think of us as a less tech-savvy firm than our competition? That would be a sad day given our personal backgrounds.

We did not reach a conclusion that day, but at least the compelling reasons to double down on only tech investing were laid out. There was a broader consensus that day that the complete shift to 'consumer tech' was not too far in the future.

The market was at India's doorstep. There was a new class of founders who had had at least their last job at a start-up, compared to founders with zero tech start-up experience. Far more Indian consumers were now online. Unlike the linear growth of physical stores, business models could now expect to scale faster.

Our limited partners liked our renewed focus on technology. Investors in VC funds belong to a category called 'alternative investors'. They are super-selective and usually evaluate their decisions assuming that they will be supporting VCs over at least a decade. They lay very high emphasis on the team's track record of working together. The team dynamics in VC determine the quality of thinking in the firm. How the team's thoughts are amalgamated to capture multiple dimensions leads to better outcomes. There is also a continuity aspect—assuming VC firms are doing this right, they have arrived at a repeatable model to fund the top start-ups. The IP around repeatability is the value that limited partners look for in VC firms. Helion had at least five successful start-ups by 2012, demonstrating repeatability in backing winners.

Around the same time, several Asia-focused fund-of-fund vehicles (FOFs) had successfully raised their new funds—much bigger in size than their previous funds. These FoFs are platforms that only deploy capital into VC funds and PE funds. The big pools of capital in the world, like pension funds, with hundreds of billions of dollars, need

FoFs to help them identify the right fund managers around the world.

China venture activity had come crashing down and companies there were raising capital at huge haircuts from their last-round valuation. The environment was not as bad as in 2008, but global investors were worried about the VC train hitting a wall. Europe had its own issues, with Greece and Italy doddering under debt. The US credit rating was downgraded for the first time by Standard and Poor.

We started talking to investors in the summer of 2011. We had set our new fund size at $250 million. This had been arrived at after long deliberations—we had to be sure that we would be able to deploy about $200 million in the next three years. We were confident in our ability to deploy—we had been able to find and invest in seven to eight companies every year in the last five years. The start-ups were growing fast and most of them needed more capital. So we settled on the fund size and began our meetings with investors.

We were a 'running platform', a team that had worked together over two funds. A portfolio in place and an existing set of investors. This status is considered to be a relatively 'safe' exposure to alternate investors compared to first-time funds. The MakeMyTrip IPO had put us in a very attractive place. We had returned a profit to our investors. Not many funds had accomplished this in 2012.

We had concluded our fundraising by the end of 2011. It didn't feel like a milestone. As a firm, we rarely celebrated our successes. Celebrating successes is important, in hindsight.

It underlines the rarity of the event and induces a certain gratitude for the outcome. Our investors had trusted our firm as a credible team with an impressive track record. Limited partners lay an incredible amount of emphasis on continuity because their capital has to be managed over a ten-year period, and since it goes into a portfolio of illiquid assets, they look for teams who can manage the portfolio until it can be sold and cash can be returned.

The fund was our largest till date—$250 million in dry powder. Ready to go to the most deserving start-ups. We were in pole position as a VC.

Going all out to exploit this opportunity, we rejigged the team design. We split the opportunities among ourselves and made sure that each of us was in charge end-to-end—from defining which areas we would like to invest in to finding exciting start-ups in our areas. This would ensure that we would cover most of the opportunities in our select areas. Each focus area was covered by a tag team, which included two people from the investment team and an analyst. So far, the junior members of the team had alternated between the diverse sectors that we had been investing in. The constant moving around had prevented the team from developing specializations. Now, with this focus, each member of the team was tasked with becoming an expert. They were supposed to know the dynamics of the market, intimately know the key start-ups and also network with people from the industry who could validate or dispute their assumptions.

Our teams split responsibility for covering the wide spectrum of angels. The angel community expanded most rapidly from

2011 to 2015. One hundred and fifty companies were funded by angels in 2011 compared to 650 in 2015. For VCs, these angel-funded companies were hot property because they had received some capital to advance their plan. Some were considered to be of high enough quality to have made an angel write a cheque. There was a pecking order. So mapping angels and seed funds had become important.

I invested in seven companies over Funds One and Two. This was about an investment a year. I had been learning a lot of lessons about start-up behaviour in India. In 2012, I felt better about deploying venture money than ever before. My network and relationships were strong. I could access and connect with founders. I was looking for moats that start-ups could build around their business. I was also mindful of growth fuelled only by investor capital. A transaction business is a straightforward business—count the shipments as they go out of the door. But if it's built only on spending investor money to acquire customers, then it cannot sustain itself. How can the start-up attract customers without burning a dollar every time? What is the repeatable advantage that only this start-up had—a 'moat' that prevented the business from being replicated quickly by a rival? How do companies build bigger 'moats'?

The year 2012 was surprisingly slow for us. We were still investing our last few deals from Fund Two and the work on the themes for Fund Three meant we had to complete our internal exercise.

I spent a lot of time on a payment company that was aimed at solving the trust gap in online marketplaces. Introduced to me by Rajan Mehra, who had run eBay India and now ran Nirvana Advisors in Mumbai, this start-up called EPay was still a paper plan. Rajan had worked with the founders at eBay.

The two founders, A and B, lived in Mumbai. A had run a payment product inside eBay. B had just quit eBay, where he had run marketing. eBay is a marketplace in which the buyer and the seller have low confidence in each other and need a third party to make sure that transactions go through by creating a layer of trust. The buyer should be satisfied with the purchase. The seller should get his money if the buyer is happy.

I respected Rajan's acumen in backing fresh new businesses. He had a strong sense of market gaps in India that he had seen first-hand while running eBay's India business. eBay was early in India, as it was in China. Like Uber, it had also faced serious local competition. Alibaba had beaten it down from the number one spot for Chinese exporters. eBay India had not faced such tight competition and built a small but sustainable business in India.

It had produced a strong 'mafia', with at least four VCs coming out from the leadership team and three well-known start-ups, at last count.

When Rajan sent me a mail about EPay on 15 October 2012, I was all over it. Rajan knew me as one of the few other investors who understood opportunities in payments. We had looked at some payment companies in the past and often discussed how the market was evolving. With Rajan as a co-investor, I was confident that we would make good partners to help build a business.

Within three days of the introduction, I had spent enough time with the founders to have a basic sense of the plan and their background. In low-trust marketplaces, transactions required a third party to adjudicate the exchange. Holding the payment in a neutral 'escrow' was a strong deterrent to fraudulent trades. There was no global precedence to an escrow company that was independent from the mothership—usually a large online marketplace. Alibaba had Alipay. eBay had its own. Would India be a long tail e-commerce marketplace where the payment operation was an expert function best left to a specialist like EPay?

I introduced the business to some of our portfolio companies, like Hoopos and Fashionara. We wanted to check their reaction to EPay's pitch. Would they value the offering? I wrote to larger marketplaces like Snapdeal to check the hypothesis. We also fixed up calls with Flipkart and Myntra.

A very helpful practice at Helion was each of the partners writing their weekly report to share with everyone on the team. This report laid out the priorities for the partner, flagged important deals and mentioned what help they needed. On 29 October, I assigned high priority to EPay, indicating that this was a company I was taking a very serious look at. As it happens in most start-ups, the future roles of the founders are not defined. There is an unspoken understanding that leaves a loose arrangement of who the ultimate voice is. For start-ups that have more than one founder equally vested in the success, it's hard to tell which one of them would die on the post. Between the EPay founders, that conversation had perhaps not reached a conclusion. As investors who wrote large cheques, we wanted this clarity. We were decently connected to the eBay network and the broader e-commerce ecosystem and could perform thorough diligence on the team and business value proposition.

We went on a calling spree. One purpose was to understand the founders, A and B, as people, their strengths and weaknesses. The second purpose of the call was to talk to marketplaces to check on their comfort to outsource the 'escrow' function. These online commerce players had heard the pitches from both founders. The smaller online merchants we spoke to were keen to use them, but to most of the large commerce businesses, payment was an important function to 'own'. Using a vendor for a value-added function was a discomfort—'We would rather build it in-house' was the common feedback from them.

The takeaway on the founders was that Founder A was the product specialist and could build a reliable escrow that customers would trust. He had done it at eBay and knew the mechanics better than anyone else.

Founder B was considered to be very strategic in his partnership conversations. This product needed a partnership more than a sale.

4 November 2012 was a Sunday. Our team had just finished a quarterly review meeting in Bangalore and were all in town on Monday. We decided to move fast to use this time to have the founders meet the Helion team. A smaller group spent four hours in our office with the founders, who came down from Mumbai. The next day, at 8.30 a.m., we had them sitting in

front of all seven members of our investment team. Everyone liked the idea but there was a strong opinion around the table. Everyone saw Founder B as the CEO. This had validated the feedback from potential customers that Founder B seemed to bring in the strategic view in the partnership conversation. This clarity, though premature, made a lot of sense.

We went back to the founders and conveyed this thought— the company would be better off with Founder B as CEO and Founder A as head of products and operations. We conveyed our thoughts to Rajan. He was a mentor to both founders and was the right person to consider this suggestion. Rajan was in agreement and conveyed our thoughts to the founders. Rajan had one additional thought that made a lot of sense— we shouldn't complicate life with fancy titles, but in essence, Founder B should lead. The next day, 8 November, Founder A came down with a fever which he suspected was dengue. We were waiting to know more about their reaction but his illness meant that we would have to wait. Rajan felt that they would be fine with this arrangement. In the meantime, we kept the internal work going. Nats wanted to know whether we were going to fund any new company before the year was out. I told him to pencil in EPay. Founder A took a week to recover. The founders got back to Rajan on 15 November. They were ready to go ahead with the change.

The two founders had agreed to the new roles: Founder B as CEO and Founder A as COO. We were also ready to go ahead. In our case, we had to take the next step. Nats opened the legal agreement discussion with Rajan's fund, Nirvana.

Breaking from the standard practice of signing a term sheet first and then moving to the lengthier legal agreements, here, we moved straight to the full legal agreements.

The founders wanted some waivers on selling their stock earlier than investors. This was a standard condition in case investors needed to exit their holding in the company. Nothing extraordinary. I started chatting with Founder B about a ninety-day plan of execution—which merchants we should focus on and try to bring on board.

On 22 November, Founder A decided that he didn't want to do it any more. He informed Rajan that he was not ready for the transition. Rajan and Founder B decided to stay focused on the opportunity and look for a co-founder. So far, we had moved fast as an investment team. We had all pitched in to get feedback and build a common understanding and an informed conclusion. But losing a co-founder who was the main product architect was too significant a change. While Founder A did his soul-searching, we also did ours. Did we cause this? Did we dodge a bullet? Wouldn't it have been worse if Founder A had decided to quit after we had funded the company? We would never know for sure, but a founder who is able to conclude that they are not willing to commit for the long term before taking an investment is far more desirable than one who decides later.

12

As per the plan for our third fund, we were being deliberate rather than reactive about investing. Defining the thesis would help because we would be able to consider the entire opportunity set and pick the areas that suited us better instead of randomly jumping all over the map, causing regrets in the future. My thesis area was 'mobility' or the mobile-first space, where companies were building consumer and enterprise applications for the new world of mobiles as the primary device.

I had to update my understanding of new-age mobility companies. In fact, our first internal deck was an effort only to educate our team that the world of mobile value-added services (VAS) and the world of mobility companies were separate. Mobility was a fundamentally new way of thinking about products that combined with the unique processing power of a mobile phone.

I started to reach out to my network in Silicon Valley. Twitter had been around for six years and, as a mobile-first company, was one of the companies in my sight. I got a lucky break meeting Parakram Khandpur, an IIT Delhi grad who was frequently in Delhi to meet and hire students from his alma mater. He worked as a product manager at Twitter's San Francisco headquarters. A JEE 33 ranker, Parakram was right in the middle of the action at Twitter's growth team. Back in 2012, not many people understood how product management could help grow users. In India, we had not gone beyond incentive to drive adoption. Install the product and get Rs 50 worth of talktime, free, free, free. Parakram provided me with solid direction to grow my knowledge of how Silicon Valley folks were thinking about mobility. Twitter was looking to build a team in India. They also wanted to understand how to grow usage in India.

I was evaluating an investment in a company located in Hyderabad, focused on helping local businesses build an online presence using the mobile phone. I asked Parakram for his views. The feedback centred my thinking on the product—the technical challenge of being able to map what's relevant for a user based on their interest graph. Building the right growth mechanics into the product and leveraging them to grow user base. This sophistication of product-led thinking was new in India and in my thesis I started laying a lot of emphasis on team capabilities that included mobile-first product thinking.

The other big favour Parakram did me was to introduce me to Ankur Jain. Ankur was also an IIT Delhi grad and was working as a principal at Blumberg Capital, an early-stage firm in San Francisco. I met Ankur in August 2012 at his office on Market Street. We struck up an instant friendship in the meeting. However, before that, while I sat in the reception waiting for Ankur, I overheard a very interesting problem being discussed with a vendor by one of the investment staff. He explained to the vendor that as a VC firm, they wanted to help their portfolio companies with a network in which useful contacts could be found from across the entire team. VC firms in the Valley were beginning to think of themselves as networks—as operating engines that their portfolio could plug into and leverage. Providing value to the portfolio was beginning to get sophisticated! Ankur and I had a long chat on mobility. He was sitting in the Valley and getting higher-quality deal flow from India than what we were seeing! The reason was that a class of founders, who had justifiably concluded that Indian VCs did not understand or value product thinking, felt it was more worthwhile to pitch directly to US VCs. Ankur had mentioned an Indian founder who was taking an exceptional approach to building a blogging site dedicated to recipes. After I got back from the US, Ankur went incommunicado for a month. He had been swamped after the birth of his first child. He resurfaced at the end of September and introduced me to Cherian, co-founder of a food blogging site called CucumberTown. Cherian lived in Bangalore, where he worked for a gaming company called Zynga. Zynga was the creator of the hugely popular online game FarmVille. Cherian worked to solve engineering problems for several of their most popular games.

Cherian responded on email to Ankur's introduction.

I am pasting Cherian's mail verbatim because it expressed his passion for what he was building and it made an immediate impression on my mind about the person behind the mail.

This product is a conglomeration of my ideas over a period of three years plus. As such, there is a lot of research that has gone into this. Would love to take you through it. This is a story of four people in three continents, three of whom have never seen each other, building an amazing product with a singular focus to make the experience happy.

I'll be returning to Bangalore by 16 October. Would appreciate if I can spend some time with you in the weeks to come. You'll love the product and the thought process in building the landscape, the retention, engagement metrics etc.

CucumberTown had raised a $3,00,000 bridge from many prominent Silicon Valley angels like Dhiraj Rajaram and Naval Ravikant. These angels spent considerable time advising Cherian. This ensured good advice, local support in Silicon Valley and access to product talent. Cherian was looking for another $3,00,000. Ankur at Blumberg was also working on figuring out if they should invest.

I met Cherian in our Bangalore office. He was intense. Speaking slowly and deliberately, he was a living example of the community he was trying to build. He talked like a missionary about the unmet needs of passionate foodies who want to be feted by their brethren, and who took food equally seriously. Food was global. Talking about it, showing how it was made, posting pictures—all this was a serious pursuit for the developed world and the elite in the developing world.

Cherian was clearly living and breathing the product, and through pure persistence, had gotten very high-quality people to collaborate across continents to craft the product. These included a product expert from Reddit in the US and the head of a top design company in Switzerland. He showed me his study of how recipes had been captured since the olden days. I had not come across someone for whom thinking about his customers was religion. Cherian told me about the deficiencies in generic blogging sites and why recipes needed a custom product. The business idea was to build a globally acceptable product for home chefs and then help them monetize the traffic that came to read about the 'beautifully written recipes'.

Ashish and I met Cherian again and talked to him about how he planned to build for the US consumer sitting in India. He was going to move to the US and interact with the community. The US was more evolved in terms of communities that pursued common interests. Engaging with customers would not be like looking for a needle in a haystack, which it would be in India.

We had to get some independent feedback on the product thinking from a likely user who also knew about the alternatives in the market. Did someone who was Cherian's ideal customer actually want to use a product like CucumberTown?

I got feedback from Tania, my friend Mike Brown's wife in San Francisco. Tania was a home chef and kept abreast of 'foodtech'. Coincidentally, Blumberg had also reached out to Tania to get feedback about CucumberTown. Tania was sceptical about the idea that regular blogging sites had a deficiency that needed to be fixed. She felt they were good enough. She felt that the space for user-generated recipes was crowded already. However, she concluded that food bloggers who were not already very famous would like to present their content better and would need support monetizing the traffic on their sites.

Interestingly, she particularly mentioned that she found the name CucumberTown 'corny'. This was the gap between US customers and an Indian founder's social context! We spoke to some other people in the US who had a background similar to Tania's. They felt that the viral aspect of recipe sites was an opportunity and low-traffic bloggers would like to use CucumberTown.

It was a small cheque that would be added to the angel cheque of $3,00,000. We wired our funds to the company on 31 December 2012. Blumberg did not participate. CucumberTown was the first investment from our third fund.

2013 was to be a regular year. We were back to our usual pace of seven new investments during the year.

13

Sandeep Agarwal was an equity analyst with an American west coast investment bank when I first met him in 2010. He had grown up in Chandigarh and after college in India had headed to the US for his MBA. He'd had to work very hard to make his way up and effect the non-traditional career move for a desi in the US to switch from being a techie to a banker.

The MakeMyTrip IPO piqued the interest of US investment banks in the India Internet story. Sandeep was in India to look for business for his firm. He was someone I knew vaguely through common friends when we used to live in the Bay Area. When we met at the Helion office, he passed around three iPads so that we could go over the presentation conveniently. We were quite thrilled with the experience of using the cool new screens. His bank was quite small but had played a role in some of the recent tech IPOs in the US. Sandeep was high-energy throughout. He became even more passionate when he started talking about what he had seen in China. He talked endlessly about the Alibaba-owned marketplace called TaoBao. TaoBao had brought together consumers and the long tail of merchants in China by killing eBay China and taking the lion's share of online commerce in that country. In addition to the business model, there was also a strong visualization to build a culture of the little people coming together to fight the big outsider. The hard-working ant emblazoned on a flag brought the TaoBao united army to the battlefield. Sandeep loved the symbolization and applied his analytical brain to understanding the marketplace dynamics that had worked so well in China.

Within a year of our meeting, Sandeep quit his banking job, moved to India and co-founded ShopClues, a marketplace along the lines of TaoBao, with an investment of $2,50,000 from his personal funds. He went about hiring a team and raised his first round of investment from angels. In January 2012, three months after launching a closed trial site, Nexus Ventures led the Series A round. Sandeep had reached out to me for investing, but I was wary about a founder who had just returned from the US to build a transaction-heavy business in India.

We wanted some evidence of execution prowess and that did not take too long. By October of 2012, Sandeep was back in the market for a second round. The business was showing solid growth—in the ten months of operations, monthly transactions had grown to 3500 and the annualized gross merchandise value was Rs 60 crore. More than 1000 sellers had listed 55,000 items for sale on the marketplace. By focusing on a category of goods that are 'brand-less', like buckets, slippers and hair clips, ShopClues could play on deeper margins. The past ten months had been superlative, and Sandeep had proven that he could execute in the Indian environment. We were aware of the high cash burn that other e-commerce companies were engaging in to keep the growth momentum. Customers were acquired for as high as Rs 3000 to Rs 5000 for the first transaction. The stakes were high, so this crazy cost was not entirely without reason. In contrast, ShopClues was spending less than Rs 500 to close a transaction.

This cash efficiency was so stark that we almost had a hard time accepting it. The model was truly catering to the long tail and had chosen a category of goods that had been ignored by Flipkart, Amazon and Snapdeal. We decided to lead the Series B round and ShopClues became our first horizontal e-commerce investment.

During this period, my personal quest to find exciting investments was leading me to talk to new friends like Parakram and Ankur and old friends from college.

Investment opportunities come from diverse connects, and personal networks play a big role in what a VC looks at. After finishing school at St Joseph's Academy in Dehradun, I went to study at BITS, Pilani.

I was fairly well-connected to students ahead of me and in my junior batch. My wife being a year junior to me in BITS also added to my proximity to the junior batch.

Sunil was a batch behind me in BITS. In early 2012, he called me to catch up. Sunil had led India sales for several technology product companies and had recently started representing a late-stage start-up. He used to closely track enterprise software vendors in India. He asked me if I was interested in investing in an enterprise security company. I had worked with several in the US and so had a decent sense of the problems that needed to be solved. Sunil told me to check out a company called Seclore. He also suggested I speak to another person we knew from BITS who ran a consulting company for enterprise security in Pune. Both conversations were intriguing enough to get me curious to know more about Seclore.

I decided to meet the founders, Vishal and Abhijit. Vishal was an IIT Bombay graduate who was on his second start-up with Seclore. The first one was sold for a nominal price. Vishal was a national swimming champion and had an interesting lineage. His grandfather was 'the Mr Agarwal' of Agarwal Classes—the original IIT prep course used by lakhs of IIT aspirants, including myself. Abhijit was a graduate from IIT Kharagpur. Seclore was based in Mumbai.

Vishal was a frequent visitor to Gurgaon. He and I first met in early 2012. Vishal was leading sales himself and had been building the business on shoestring funding and revenue from the business. He was down-to-earth, with a good sense of humour. He and I hit it off immediately. Vishal had also studied at St Joseph's Academy in Dehradun when his father was transferred there from Lucknow. We had some good laughs remembering the odd characters at school. Vishal told me about his journey with his previous start-up and how he came to found Seclore.

Seclore had built a sophisticated Information Rights Management (IRM) product that allowed companies to protect their files, especially those sent to people outside the company. Bring your own device, or BYOD, was fuelling the problem of unprotected file sharing. Protecting information leaving the perimeter of an enterprise was a high priority for the chief information officer.

Till the mid-nineties, IRM was considered by large US corporations to be a panacea for the problem of files landing in the wrong hands. Customers had high expectations from it. Many large corporations bought expensive licenses and started implementing the system. These products were so complex that the implementation dragged on and on. After many millions of dollars, the complexity increased to a point that these products couldn't be used any more. They had to be thrown out, leaving a bad taste in the mouth for many. Most solutions had very complex integration problems, because large enterprises were like spaghetti when it came to file formats. Seclore was designed from the ground up to solve this complexity of implementation. Solving this problem from India was natural because the product needed massive integration code, and more importantly because no one would fund another IRM company in the US.

Seclore was competitively priced but not cheap. Vishal was a good mix of sales and technology. He did a good job in positioning the product as the Rolls Royce of IRM and also highlighted the ease of implementation. We stayed in touch. I used to drop in to the Mumbai office to catch up and Vishal would do the same in Gurgaon. They didn't need any immediate capital and I was the only VC talking to them at this point.

Tenet Fund, a seed-stage fund, was the only investor in Seclore. Sateesh Andra was managing the fund. We knew each other from the Bay Area, where I had been involved in acquiring a business that Sateesh had co-founded. Seclore certainly didn't have the cash to try anything exciting. My own thesis about enterprise software products in India was that the Indian market was meant to provide a validation and help improve the product for a global launch. India's IT spend was not enough to justify funding a company that relied only on Indian customers. So my big question was, 'Can Vishal sell to global customers?' Would global customers choose an Indian company's software to protect their digital assets?

I started working to get an answer to this question. At that time, Seclore had a few customers in Germany and Singapore. I called my network in the Bay Area. I reached out to people running security companies and VCs who invested in security for large corporations.

Just like UnitedLex, this was a check on whether the market existed in the right geography. If the answer was yes, then we could help Seclore grow into these markets and build one of the first global enterprise software companies from India.

Seclore started off as a casual conversation but matured into a formal fundraise. The best part of the transaction was the time we got to understand the space and track the progress. In October 2012, Vishal appointed a banker in India to help with the fundraise. The plan was to raise $5 million to help him hire and grow outside India. We had finished our diligence by the time the banker came on board. So, without wasting more time, we gave a term sheet for an investment in Seclore.

We considered co-investing in the round with a VC from California, which would provide a bridge to Seclore becoming a Silicon Valley company. The feedback we got from the VCs who met Vishal was that they liked him, but were still jaded by the past disappointment in IRM. They were also not willing to go through the regulatory complexity of investing in an Indian company. Seclore would have got access to key US hires and customers if this had worked out. The quality of VC has a strong bearing on the quality of people who associate with a company in the Bay area. Hyderabad-based Ventureast also knew the company through its associate fund, Tenet. We decided to give a term sheet together with Ventureast.

The most important element of the shareholding structure of a start-up is the ownership held by the founders. In companies that give away too much too early, investors who come in later often worry that founders with low ownership may not remain motivated in the long run. This worry is often superseded by the enthusiasm of investing in a new company, but it usually comes back to haunt investors.

Seclore's seed investors had taken a big bite very early in the company for a small investment. So I had a chat with Vishal on whether we should first fix this imbalance. Vishal had been promised some equity back if he delivered performance, but through a mix of delay in performance and complex regulations, the equity earn-back was not possible. Vishal, like most founders, told us that they were satisfied with their ownership and we should go ahead.

We thought of giving a valuation that was three times the sales booking for the year. In a complex three-way tug-of-war, which included giving minimum ownership to the two investors, giving enough money for the company to execute and stipulating that the founders not have their ownership reduced even further, we settled on a price that was 20 per cent higher than planned. The funding decision was followed by the terms of the investment.

In 2012, enterprise software companies had limited expectations of ever issuing an IPO. The more likely scenario was a sale to a larger company in a strategic acquisition. Real-life examples were few, and the ones that happened were not more than $50 million in size.

The timing of exit from enterprise software companies was notoriously important. We had also seen that when an acquirer came along, it was not always a wise idea to ignore the offer just because the valuation was not appealing. Acquirers knocking on any company's door was a remarkable combination of fortuitous timing and luck. It didn't happen very often. Normally, a company has to go looking for a buyer, and the odds of finding a buyer are higher compared to when buyers come calling.

One of our outsourcing companies had an inbound offer to get acquired at $100 million. We pooh-poohed the offer and opted to stay put, smugly assuming that there would be bigger offers in the future. No one ever came. That price was the high mark in the history of the company, an offer we should have grabbed with both hands.

In Seclore's case, we were the investors who came in for the long haul without beating down the entry price. We faced the quandary of either becoming a reluctant seller in a sub-optimal acquisition offer or ignoring one and then missing the only window for a sale.

The legal solution to this was adding some ingenuity to a standard clause called the liquidation preference. This clause allowed paying out preferred shareholders over and above the proceeds from a regular sale of shares. We asked Vishal for a liquidation preference in case the company was eventually sold for a value that was below what would make the cut for a nominal return for us. Selling above that number would not attract any special exit value for us. So if the company sold for $150 million and at that value we were not able to make our desired return, we would be given preference to get our return ahead of other shareholders.

With the legal terms now on the table, Vishal and I were no longer having relaxed, forward-looking discussions—we were fighting over every point. Vishal had the insecurity of running a company where investors held majority. The negotiations would turn into fights. Our lawyers were trying their best to sort through the new requirements for protection being thrown at them.

Vishal's goal was to have an end event beyond which the rights that investors were getting would fall off. The liquidation preference would not be applicable in multiple scenarios. With our lawyers' relentless push, we all agreed to the terms of the investment and after three months of intense negotiation we became the largest shareholders in Seclore.

My last few investments had been as a forty-year-old. I was meeting more founders younger to me than before. I was still being confused for a much younger person because of how I looked. I had gone through the stress of Getit's lack of progress and the crisis at Spandana. I had met enough Indian start-up founders to build a good framework to assess and compare. I had negotiated enough agreements to know what to give up on and what to focus on. I was no longer afraid to fail. This was a good place to be in for my next decade.

14

On 5 July 2013, Apoorv Sharma of Venture Nursery sent me a mail connecting me to the founder of a company called Oravel that they had seed-funded.

The founder, Ritesh, wrote me a nice short mail introducing himself.

Oravel operated a private-label, no-frills, standardized network of rooms at 'half the price of a hotel'. Ritesh described his company as a 'private-label affiliate that had been started recently and [which] is becoming users' favourite for budget stays'. His mail was an eye-catcher in which he precisely captured the key points of what they did, how they had been growing, their credentials and when they would like to raise their next round,

Since its seed round, Oravel had grown to employing seventeen people, with six of them owning equity. Revenue had grown ten times between December 2012 and April 2013. He was already thinking of scaling up growth because he talked about API-based distribution partnerships with online travel operators.

Ritesh was nineteen years old at that time. He was a Thiel Fellow, which explained his having a start-up at that age. To get started, he had raised seed funding a year back and had used it to prove the model. Now he was trying to reach out to VCs and was keen to close his funding in a month or two. In any market, nineteen is an unusually young age to start a business—even Mark Zuckerberg was shy of his twentieth birthday when he brought Facebook to Silicon Valley investors. That a nineteen-year-old in India could start a business and raise seed capital was a testimony to the growing risk-taking capacity among Indian investors.

I introduced Ritesh to my colleague who was covering travel. He had met Ritesh earlier but still did a perfunctory catch-up. The age factor was an oversized oddity. The ability of a nineteen-year-old to build a business was highly questionable.

Oravel did not even make it to the priority list in our internal filter. Better known as OYO, Oravel would be running 12,000 hotels in 337 cities by 2019 and would be valued at $5 billion.

The age of the average founder had been shifting downwards in the 2012–14 period. We had backed young founders with their refreshing views of the world. There was a perpetual debate on whether experience made any difference in founding a start-up. What are the key skills that a founder needs that come only with age? Perhaps knowing how to deal with failures better, having seen more with age? In Ritesh's case, he would make mistakes, but so would everyone when figuring out a new business model. Do young founders have a lower opportunity cost? Opportunity cost is what a founder would lose while pursuing the dream. Younger founders are quick to say that if their start-up fails, they can always go back and get a job, while a founder in his mid-thirties could risk prematurely ending a fast-growth career if he were to step out and start a company.

Would fear of failure drive the founder?

My view is that once a founder gets going, the life energy that is infused into getting a business off the ground, combined with the ability to envision the future, is independent of age. Most founders are not weighing options and in reality they know that the life they lived before becoming a founder has been left behind.

By the summer of 2013, Hoopos, the online baby product company, had been around for more than a year and a half. The orders were trickling in and despite maintaining a high standard of customer responsiveness the order growth was not looking like there was a big market pull. Across all baby commerce companies, growth had been disappointing. It was a category that theoretically should have been growing much faster. Parents in India were as doting as new parents in China. Why weren't they spending? Cost consciousness was a big factor—prices still drove parents when they bought goods.

A dream investment for a VC is of course the one where a small first check can throw up conclusive evidence of the business having wings or not. This would be a strong reason for a VC to decide to invest more capital in that company. In

Hoopos, the first check had been inconclusive, so we had to invest some more. Once again, we were the only investors.

Raising more capital didn't seem easy. Deep pockets were needed to build a category, but there was little evidence that a standalone business could be built. So we needed to go with the view that the company could last long enough.

Meanwhile, Accel's investment, BabyOye, had consumed a similar amount of capital but had grown faster than Hoopos. They had used a loss leader, diapers, to scale the orders, but the repeat purchase rates of Hoopos were higher.

The number of orders for both of them was quite small. We had met both companies in their formative days, so we also knew the founders of BabyOye. They were from a large company background. So far, they had kept a good handle on operations. Accel, Helion and Tiger had partnered earlier and they could carry a business forward with the combined investment firepower.

We started exploring a merger with BabyOye. The merger would give some scale and bring the combined company at par with FirstCry, which was rumoured to be at 1000 orders a day at that time.

15

We invested in RedBus in 2011 and then again in 2012. Phani had been growing up on lessons that he was learning in the hot seat as the CEO. The role can be a tough one, with a person expected to look beyond old relationships and 'being a nice guy'. Investors and the board demand that the CEO prioritize doing what is best for the business. Tough actions usually don't help you win the popularity contest. Emotionally, it can be painful to cause distress to so many people who have been loyal to your mission in the early days. Growth was strong—the company was now selling tickets worth Rs 100 crore a month.

Phani had recently brought on board four senior hires—heads of marketing and HR, a CFO and a product head. Each of them brought solid learning and they were all excited to drive the company's growth over the next few years.

Bus ticketing had grown in volumes and RedBus had also opened connections from their software to other applications

(APIs) for other online travel agents, so tickets were being sold from redbus.com as well as multiple other websites.

All this with a total funding of less than $10 million!

Like Vishal at Seclore, Phani had also raised early-stage capital at a high dilution, leaving him running a company where investors held a majority stake.

In early 2013, the company had appointed a top banker to raise capital to fund growth. With a strong team and growth, the board was confident of a successful raise. RedBus had raised its seed capital in 2006. Helion had invested in 2011 with the expectation that the company would continue to grow manifold over the next few years. When VCs invest, they care a lot about the multiple on their capital—they budget for five-six years before they get returns—but the objective is to make at least five-ten times return in five years. So as a start-up raises capital over the years, the motivation to exit varies across the early entrants and the late entrants. This causes some tension.

The banker went out and started talking to investors. The last quarter had been slow for the company, and despite how long-term an investor has to be on a start-up's future, new investors always use the last quarter performance as an excuse to negotiate price.

Despite the slow quarter, fundraising was going well. Fundraising for start-ups is a lot like fishing for a smart game like trout. Like a skilled fisherman who waits for a bite, followed by the tug before he starts to reel in, a smart fundraiser understands the nature of each investor conversation. They wait for the tug. You tug too soon and you lose the conversation prematurely.

RedBus funding started getting tugs from several high-quality investors. A prominent VC was crafting a deal that would get them to own majority through a combination of taking ownership by buying out existing shareholders and also investing directly in the company. Another late-stage investor was serious. A large multinational technology company called MIH that had been on the periphery of travel commerce in India was also talking about a financial investment. It owned a travel site called Ibibo in India.

With enough tugs, it was time to reel in. The banker started precipitating these conversations to real offers on paper. The valuation was disappointing, as expected. Just that one quarter of slow growth had become a factor. The VCs had offered valuations that were too close, which almost seemed like something had guided them. Were they talking to each other? Hard to find out.

The conversations continued. And continued. More straightforward with the VCs, but with the strategic player, the nature of the transaction started looking very complex.

With the usual mix of certainty and uncertainty, the conversations flip-flopped between 'it's happening' and 'it's not happening'. Every time there is a strategic option, it invariably causes the interested parties to start talking about the problems and challenges more than the exciting places the company could grow to. The 'salesy' pitches are replaced by moaning about slowing growth, teams, the competition from incumbents. Depending on whether you favour a sale or not, you choose between 'the competition could kill us' and 'we could kill the competition'.

The banker was pushing for closure. They had to bring this transaction to its conclusion and cater to three investors and the founders' requirements.

Somewhere along the way, the strategic sale started gaining favour. The pricing and conditions that were being offered by the VCs was not compelling enough to argue against the sale. With all kinds of risk being thrown about to justify a near-term exit, the future did not look as bright as before. With the founders also finding that the strategic option made more sense, the needle swung completely.

Every transaction starts as a complex one. Then everyone jumps up and says, 'Oh, it's too complex. Let's keep it simple.' So, then everyone is relieved and signs off fast. By the summer of 2013, we signed off the term sheets for MIH to take a controlling interest in RedBus. In a few months, the transaction wrapped up, with shareholders receiving cash in the sale. RedBus became part of MIH, with Phani continuing as CEO. We made decent returns, but had the business continued to build all of us could have made a lot more. Fundraises determine the future direction for start-ups. What could have been a strong funding for future growth turned out to be an unplanned premature exit.

On 31 July 2013 we opened our inbox to read about a shocking development. Sandeep Agarwal of ShopClues had been arrested by the FBI in San Jose, California, on insider trading charges. Preet Bharara, the New York state attorney, was coming down heavily on insider trading cases. Sandeep was charged with sharing insider information on a Microsoft–Yahoo! deal with his clients. It was a big setback for ShopClues—the company had been growing rapidly and Sandeep was the driving force of the business. He had all the ideas. We had been investors for only three months and in these three months ShopClues had shown strong growth. Not in our wildest dreams could we have imagined that we would hit a wall in such a short time.

Fate can be cruel. In a blink, it can snatch away the order from our carefully planned lives and thrash them around till we stop believing in free will. The only recourse is to accept the unpredictability and be prepared for the wild swings. Sandeep was in the middle of a storm. Suddenly, with no warning, it came and took over his life. Chaos is a natural occurrence. It is waiting around the corner, we just don't know when we will make the turn. Over time, disarray, lack of arrangement and chaos always increase. This is the second law of thermodynamics, which states that 'the total entropy of an isolated system can never decrease over time'.

Why does entropy feature in a book about founders and VCs? It's found a mention here because this brilliant law offers great insight when it comes to explaining the ups and downs of human life. The amplitude of swings from 'It's all good' to 'Oh my God, I don't know what the heck just happened' hits founders frequently. It is more frequent than for any other average person. They just learn to take it in their stride and force their broken spirits to recover much faster than the rest of us.

Yvon Chouinard, the founder of Patagonia, has said, 'The hardest thing in the world is to simplify your life because everything is pulling you to be more and more complex.'

Humans strive all their lives to bring about order by fighting back the natural effects of chaos. However, when people understand that this predictable chaos is the cause of their life's upheavals and not a result of what other people are doing, then their ability to recover from the mess is enhanced dramatically.

Good entrepreneurs bounce back like good sportspersons. That is because their daily highs and lows make them better at dealing with this chaos that start-ups keep going through. At Helion, we firmly believed that all start-ups would go through at least one near-death experience. Especially those destined for greatness.

Events like Sandeep's arrest or Spandana's ban seem cataclysmic when they occur. Both companies survived these events and went on to become bigger. They just needed to believe in their purpose. They restored order and stayed alert for the next blow. The blows never go away.

Sandeep's situation with the US Department of Justice was unpredictable in terms of both time and outcome.

For an accelerating company like ShopClues, which needed to continue raising capital from global investors, every day of remaining in an unpredictable situation was fraught with risk. The company needed to be stable. Everyone went into a huddle to figure out the best path forward.

Sanjay Sethi had moved back to India with Sandeep as co-founder of ShopClues. Sanjay used to be the global product head for shipping and logistics, payments and billing at eBay. A contrasting personality to Sandeep's gregarious one, Sanjay was quiet and collected. He was happily doing what he knew best until the wheel of fate turned that day and put the spotlight on him. Closely involved with Sandeep from the early days, Sanjay was best placed to bring stability to a rocking boat. Once it was established that Sandeep was not coming back to India in the short term, the board appointed Sanjay as the CEO.

The Hoopos merger discussion with BabyOye was still on. The Helion partnership had an intense debate on the question of Hoopos' future. The merger would mean that Helion became a shareholder in the combined entity. We had to have an unflinching belief that a start-up that could be a leader in the baby commerce vertical would fetch good returns for us. The partnership was divided on it based on the evidence we had so far.

We had also never seen a merger of start-ups that had worked. The odds were stacked high against a successful outcome. The partnership had discussed the issues threadbare. There was no fact hidden from anyone—it was a debate in which we all were aware of the challenges as well as the positives. An example of what we at Helion liked to call 'being intellectually honest'. We could have had a debate without the facts—people could still have a negative view but they would be imagining most of it. Even worse, we could have debated without such a stark view of the challenges and an unrealistic sense of optimism would have pervaded the discussion. In VC discussions where there is a lot of future-gazing and people extrapolating based on past experiences, fear belongs to the people who are not close to the company and optimism belongs to the ones who are. Conviction alone can put an end to the debate. The opposing viewpoints were put to rest and we proceeded to give it a shot.

The Hoopos–BabyOye merger was on. There were two levels of discussion—what the new founder team would look like, and how the three investors would support the merged business. The teams had decided their roles and agreed that a merger was best for everyone. It was decided that Sanjay, the CEO of BabyOye, would run the business post-merger. The investor base would strengthen. The combined business would have higher revenue and more rationalized costs. With Helion, Accel and Tiger, the merged entity would have a decent shot at making a play to be number one or two in the baby care e-commerce space. Merging two start-ups with their own sets of shareholders was harder than it looked. It was an intense project for the finance teams. The transaction needed many loose ends to be tied up before it eventually became official.

16

Venture capital as an asset class is considered by global investors to be in the highest risk bracket. When large investors decide how much to invest in venture capital, they usually think of less than 5 per cent of their total pool. Venture capital receives a far smaller allocation of capital when compared to public markets, private equity and real assets. Venture capital is also the creator of the next generation of the most disruptive companies. Without venture funding, we would still be calling yellow-and-black cabs, paying for expensive hotel rooms on our family holidays after booking them through travel agents, and not being sure if we got the most suitable airline ticket. The amount of capital allocated to venture capital has been growing over the years.

Global liquidity had expanded since the 2000s, and after the 2008 monetary crisis, major central banks had flooded the developed market with more money. 'The money supply of the G4 (the United States, the United Kingdom, the Euro area and

Japan)—a proxy for global liquidity—rose from $18 trillion in 2003 to $35 trillion in 2014. Foreign exchange reserves—a proxy for official liquidity—increased four-fold from $3.2 trillion in 2003 to over $12 trillion in 2014,' as per an IMF working paper.[2]

From 2014 onwards, deployments in venture capital across the US and China hit new highs. US VCs invested $47.3 billion across 3617 deals in 2014, 62 per cent higher than in 2013. There were many mega rounds of $500 million. The last two quarters in 2014 alone saw over $13 billion each in funding.

China followed a similar path. In 2014, Chinese VCs invested $15.5 billion, up from $5 billion in 2013—an increase of three times or an additional $10 billion for its start-ups. Most of these VC funds had raised their capital from global investors.

The year 2014 was what they call a bubble year. A spike in capital availability had caused over-allocation to venture capital. VCs had bigger funds and were also investing faster. Companies were raising fresh rounds of capital faster than before. When a VC deploys capital, price discovery is driven by a shallow buyer market of other VCs. Public markets are sophisticated in pricing efficiency because of a much higher number of buyers; VCs are far fewer in number and information is grossly asymmetric. When market sentiments are frothy, prices tend to drift away from value more acutely than in public markets.

In India, the froth started appearing in 2014 and hit a peak in 2015. In scale, it was a fraction of the US and China, but in characteristics, it took Indian start-ups through an incredibly fast pace of change. More new start-ups funded in this period will go on to become unicorns in the next three to four years, the fastest in VC history.

The two-horse race was a new phenomenon: start-ups were realizing that creating value was a zero-sum game. Start-ups would compete with each other to create gaps among themselves. VCs would come in and fund them at different points. Very quickly, leaders would start emerging and at least two would stay in the race. These two would then face off for the grand prize. It would be a well-funded fight from both sides, but it had to have only one winner. If there were two start-ups competing for leadership in the same niche, both were worse off. The threat of another late-stage investor syndicate coming together to back the competition would always be lurking. Cash would then always be considered at risk. Once the risk was removed through a merger or burnout, the last one standing was rewarded with the leadership premium. This was more common in e-commerce than in other businesses. If customers depended on only your business, they would come back again and again to buy goods from you. This would justify the high cost of acquisition of the customer.

The stage of entry for an investment firm had been easy to determine, but starting 2014, there was no telling which firm would come in at what stage. Tiger could come in at a Series A and an early-stage firm could do a Series C. Mostly it was backwards, with typical late-stage capital investors entering start-ups early in their journey. Tiger had already started entering in Series A with co-investors in 2012 in companies like LetsBuy and BabyOye, but in 2014 it started going solo in Series A investments. Tiger made a total of seventeen investments in India in 2012 and 2013.

At Helion, we had six investment partners, and we were making seven to eight investments a year. Tiger made seventeen investments in 2014 alone, with its principal sitting in New York. Many of the investments were based on referrals from existing portfolio founders.

In the middle of all this frenzy, our investment thesis on the new 'mobile everything' world was slowly emerging. We now had a broad understanding of the areas where smartphones and app stores would disrupt the world as we knew it back in 2012. We had assimilated learnings from the US and met the first few 'mobile app' companies in India. These founders were challenging mobile web companies, which did not acquire customers in as sticky a manner as a mobile app. We also learnt about the constraints of data and memory in India—apps had to be less than 5MB in size because otherwise people would uninstall them for taking too much space.

In 2012, the very first mobile app company we met was based in Bangalore. It was called DelightCircle. Shradha Sharma of YourStory had introduced us to the start-up. The CEO and co-founder was a US returnee who did not have a technology background. The other two co-founders, Ravi and Yash, were all one year out of IIT Kharagpur and still carried the emaciated engineering student look in loose, round-necked T-shirts. They had built an app that could help users locate 'deals' from retailers closest to them and guide their purchase decisions. They had signed up for a pilot with Reliance and Total Mall. I liked the guys—they were young but represented the mobile-first generation. They had learnt about mobile back end and front end while they were at IIT and had had a start-up even when they were in college. While it was fascinating and a sign of things to come, we passed on DelightCircle because it was not fitting into the natural shopping behaviour of consumers.

Time went by until the summer of 2014. An intern who was helping us with the mobile thesis had been tasked with identifying exciting start-ups working on tools that were building the mobile economy. All of them were seed stage. He had to classify them into two buckets—one where the urgency to raise was high and the second where the founders were some time away from being ready for funding. We did not want to miss the ones who were raising capital right away. The second bucket we would track, but there was no impending action. The intern strongly recommended a company called MoEngage. MoEngage's co-founders were ex-DelightCircle, Raviteja and Yash. They were both a little older and on their own now. MoEngage was born out of their lesson from DelightCircle: users uninstalled the app and the cost of winning the user went down the tube as a consequence. A tool for marketing teams at mobility start-ups, MoEngage had built a personalized notification app to prompt users. Ravi and Yash had just finished building the product and were running trials at TaxiforSure, which was a Helion portfolio company.

Our underlying thesis was that globally successful start-ups that built tools for mobility companies could be born in India. India was a mobile-first market while the US had the legacy of the desktop.

I was staying at a hotel in Bangalore that was closer to the airport, for a change, and during that trip I met Ravi again. He came by and met me for breakfast, and we talked about MoEngage. Ravi took a city bus to come see me. After a good chat, I was getting into my cab to head to the airport while Ravi walked off to catch a Bangalore city bus back to the office. He did not take up any job after graduating from IIT. He struggled with DelightCircle, and then put his head out again with MoEngage!

We got good feedback from our investee company, TaxiforSure, about the MoEngage product. TaxiforSure had been using it to prompt customers to book more cabs. The product had demonstrated an uptick for them.

We called Ravi and Yash to our office to meet our investment team. We didn't realize that for the engineering co-founder, anything before 11 a.m. was too early. Yash looked like he had been dragged out of bed by Ravi to make it to the meeting on time!

We wrote a seed cheque that would be sufficient to take the company to a Series A financing. MoEngage got selected by a US-based enterprise incubator, and the team was off to San Francisco for six months. Ravi and Yash would now work and live in San Francisco, learning the nuts and bolts of building a technology product from top entrepreneurs in the space. They would have mentors who would be able to connect them to resources that could help jump-start their growth. The world map of customers and competition seemed so distant sitting in Koramangala. Now they would live in the heart of it. They would have to adapt quickly to Silicon Valley and make the most of it.

How two struggling young founders from Koramangala could seamlessly be transported to the hip San Francisco start-up scene is what made the venture capital world so fascinating to me.

Many new start-ups in India were being formed by replicating the business models of successful start-ups from the US and China. Sometimes Indian consumers were ready and sometimes the business turned out to be too early for a diverse country like India. Food tech was a category that took a bite of this apple in several different ways. Many of these companies assumed that Indian consumers had sophisticated palates and needed to be delivered fancy food at their doorstep. The foodtech space saw more than 400 start-ups in 2015.[3] Foodtech was a hot sector in the US and China, where the per capita GDP exceeded India's $1600 by at least five times. Per capita GDP in the US was $56,000 and in China, $8000 in 2015. Yet, founders and investors backed the sector as if India were a wealthy country. Several companies that looked at gourmet food, home chef networks, organic food stores, dessert-only delivery and, of course, a fair share of food and grocery delivery businesses came up. Many founders came from a food background and had no idea about logistics or tech. They loved the idea that their passion for food could graduate to a fundable start-up.

No other sector ignored the spending power of an average Indian as much as foodtech. With only 7 million households in India earning more than $30,000 in 2017, we were woefully short of the hundreds of millions of customers needed to make the high-burn businesses viable.

What made these businesses appear successful in the US and China was the temporary traction from customers who were used to being spoilt, besides massive rounds of financing. Indian start-ups had been following and replicating American businesses with a time lag thus far. It was after the lessons from the US market were learnt that India would start to replicate. Foodtech was the first sector that was replicated, even before it was clear whether it made sense in the US.

In 2014, to have Tiger's fund back you was a prayer on every competitive founder's lips. If you had Tiger on your side, the odds of another investor getting into the ring to compete with your start-up were minimized. You could raise a lot of capital, but you wouldn't need to burn cash excessively unless you were forced to do so by another start-up that was fighting for the top spot. And if you can pull the biggest investors to your side, you create a deterrent for others based on your power to outspend the competition. Unless a large global competitor with more capital on its balance sheet appears as competition, under ideal conditions, capital can be a deterrent.

For every 'smart' investor, there is a trail of club investors who add to the pool of capital available to the companies that this investor chooses to back. These investors who follow the smart investor are maximizing their chances of winning by joining the right club. If you belong to the wrong club, you could find yourself struggling to convince late-stage investors to back your company. TaxiforSure versus Ola was a skirmish like this. Investors were throwing in the towel after simply reading the shareholder lists of the two competitors. It was the one and only perfect information in a two-horse race. TaxiforSure raised its seed capital from Helion and Accel. Tiger backed Ola. Ola grew faster but burnt through more cash in the process. TaxiforSure was slower but more capital-efficient. Investor psychology is looking at where capital accumulation is more likely. When TaxiforSure went out to raise growth capital under the cloud of the molestation case in an Uber cab in Delhi, investor conversations started off on a defensive note. Investors were wary of backing a company that did not look like it had a good chance to raise enough capital to compete against Ola AND Uber. Flipkart was also showing signs of weakness competing against Amazon in 2014. This was happening despite it having deep-pocketed investors. Investors wondered, 'If Flipkart, with all its capital support, can't measure up to Amazon's access to capital, how could TaxiforSure, with three Indian VCs, compete against the Uber juggernaut?'

Every round of capital that a company raises has a cost associated with it. Whether it is a loan or equity, it comes with a price tag. The price tag varies based on the risk that the provider places on the capital. When the supply of capital increases, when the comparative uses of capital are unattractive, or when the risk in the company comes down, the cost of capital is lower. When the supply shrinks, like when interest rates are tightened or when the company's prospects look shaky, the cost of capital goes up. The cost could also vary from country to country. Global capital flow to an Uber or an Amazon was far greater, and hence at a lower cost, because of the high expectations of return. Capital flow to an emerging market start-up was relatively lower and came at a higher cost. Lower-cost capital was fighting higher-cost capital and beating it convincingly through sheer size.

Early infusion of capital from deep-pocketed investors became a strong determinant of success. Do we have an investor today who can write a $100 million cheque if need be? These arguments did not give credence to the capital efficiency of the business. In 2014, capital had become both defence and offence.

17

In 2014, angels made 350 investments in which they signed cheques worth $200 million. In 2015, these angels would make 650 investments, putting out $300 million. Angels also found a formula to start clubbing their small cheques to form 'angel syndicates'. Usually, an angel would be part of a bunch of investors 'hunting in packs'. An individual would write a single cheque of Rs 10–15 lakh and then club it with five more similar-sized syndicate members' cheques.

Founders started reaching out to the most active angels. These angels were mostly founders of other successful start-ups. Their risk appetite was high and they also had a good eye for the most business-minded founders. VCs can be too intellectual in identifying businesses—these angels were more practical and liked to back founders who understood '*dhanda*'.

VCs looking for 'hot' deals started calling these founders and investing in their companies. Unicorn founders had sold a part of their own holdings to their investors and were using that money to write their angel cheques. By the time the company would raise their second or third VC round, these angel cheques would have grown handsomely in value. New investors would then offer to buy out the angels. The profits would flow to newer start-ups. This quick turnaround motivated even more angels to join in. What can be better than VCs writing large seed cheques to unproven founders? VCs writing large cheques to founders who have raised angel cheques and proven their ability to execute against competition.

The independence of capital from the domain of 'heavily engaged' VCs like Helion and the shift to hundreds of angels had one positive outcome—the broader discovery of quality entrepreneurs. The risk umbrella spread to a wider base of investors, which helped more companies raise capital. A bit like how Lata Mangeshkar's hegemony in Bollywood was loosened by the scores of unknown but talented singers emerging from talent search shows on TV.

More start-ups meant greater learning across a wider base. The VC ecosystem was finally coming of age. Learning has impact when it happens with high intensity and takes place all around us—think of it as 'Kota for start-ups'. This scale of learning over a short period of time lifted the entire VC ecosystem. Employees learnt from the founders. Founders learnt from other founders. VCs learnt from other VCs. And VC partners learnt from their VPs. Yes, even at VC firms, the senior folks learnt about the new world from the younger folks in the office.

The Internet-native generation could intuitively think of new bottles for old wine, like eating out three times a day. With the Mast Kalandar investment, we knew that young professionals needed convenient food choices, like having food delivered to their doorstep. A service that only delivered food needed tech-powered last-mile logistics. With HummingBird, we realized that unlocking unrented homes as guesthouses would create a hospitality business for corporates. Now start-ups like Swiggy and OYO were addressing the same gap with business models that catered to the digitally native consumer population.

Higher volumes of cheques meant more start-ups were at work. The scene resembled a massive nursery with lots of tiny tots, but not enough caretakers. It was Darwinian. It felt satisfyingly evolutionary for the strongest but meant quick mortality for the rest. These start-ups needed support and in some ways felt like stepchildren despite being backed by top-tier VC firms because their mortality was not as important as the Series A investments.

Work for us VCs went through the roof! No more golfing on weekdays! We were scoping, mapping and processing large numbers of opportunities.

We had to employ our gut and heuristics to sift through a much higher proportion of high-quality start-ups than before. Saying no to absolute crap is easy, but saying no to high-quality start-ups is hard. I no longer felt bored during meetings with start-ups—instead, I felt challenged.

I was forced to come prepared in the more competitive VC world. I was forced to respond faster and decide in shorter cycles. We could not afford the luxury to watch progress in start-ups over months. With VCs swooping down on unsuspecting start-ups at high speeds, we had to do our homework—we couldn't leisurely figure out the space *after* meeting a company. I had rediscovered the VC world after twelve years and the new energy was invigorating.

By 2015, VC firms had handed the chequebooks to their staff and made the seed-investing programme simple and fast. One founder was made to sign a term sheet at her apartment when junior team members from an aggressive VC firm cornered her one early morning at her doorstep to beat the rush of VCs who wanted to fund her.

VC firms invested in twenty to thirty seed-stage companies a year in 2014 and 2015. It was understood that their teams would not be able to spend as much time in company building as they would on bigger cheques. Writing seed cheques of $2,50,000 in a VC firm that typically invested $5 million needed suspension of the typical process of deliberation. Some firms were shy to invest in seeds because they did not want to overextend their ability to add value. But borders between seed funds and Series A funds were being blurred.

At some VC firm, senior partners would sponsor a $10–20 million seed cheque. This was the extremely lethal combination of stage and capital exposure. The discipline and respect for capital was an unknown trait in the founders, so trusting these early-stage start-ups with so much capital turned into a wild circus. Steve Jobs was a God to many of these founders and they made it a point to first lose their ability to listen to their investors. Then they went about town making incredible offers to employees who didn't think it necessary to make sacrifices on their pay cheque before moving to a start-up.

The move to investing in earlier-stage companies was a direct result of the fear of being priced out or missing out on future rounds. Investors were worried that good founders (read 'aggressive in raising capital') would get funded no matter what. VCs would be left out of future rounds because capital would start chasing start-ups the moment they showed some growth vectors. In slow markets, investors like to wait for more traction. Once start-ups achieve that, the investors ask for some more. Then some more and some more. There is no incentive to risk capital unless there is the fear of losing the investment to some other investor. In 2014, the behaviour turned around 180 degrees: investors were constantly jumping the gun and were taking more risk by entering investments for which they had very little proof of concept. In the VC business, the premium for risk swings from one extreme to the other. It was either too conservative or too aggressive.

~

We had to establish Helion as a thought leader in the mobile-first space. We had already connected with influencers from industry leaders like Nokia and Google and were organizing meet-ups of mobility companies in Bangalore, Mumbai and Gurgaon over beers. The process of engaging start-ups had changed—instead of sitting in our office and waiting for start-ups to be escorted in by bankers, we were out there swigging beers and talking about cross-platform app development.

Wooplr was one such company we met in March 2014. Founded by four engineers from McAfee who were as far removed from women's fashion as could be, Wooplr was one of the earliest social commerce companies in India connecting women to fashion influencers.

What we liked about Wooplr was their mobile-first approach and deep product view. It was a refreshing break from app companies that didn't talk about how the product would help drive customer adoption. Wooplr was tracking the right metrics and their growth was driven mostly by non-paid sources. Users were posting photos of themselves in their new apparel which other users would also aspire for. The app would then connect local merchants to users, who would click on a 'get it' button. Slightly convoluted, but the user-generated content engine was interesting by itself and the subsequent addition of commerce seemed possible. The newness in thinking about using the selfie-posting feature to drive user-generated content was helping the mobile-first app break away from the clutter.

Working out of a house opposite Koramangala Club, the team had done well listening to their users and translating their asks to product features.

Wooplr closed an angel investment in June 2014. By July 2014, they had a term sheet for $1 million from a large e-commerce company. This was a strategic investment for the company that was interested in Wooplr's take on social commerce. This interest was an untimely one. In a company so early in its journey, a large strategic investor was a hindrance— it would prevent financial investors from funding the business because they would doubt that the start-up would ever be able to discover its market price and hence provide the right exit to financial investors. The presence of a strategic investor who is also a potential buyer as a shareholder scares everyone off. So we didn't see this as a good development. We had to now play the dual role of convincing ourselves about investing while also watching out for the threat of losing the deal to a strategic investor.

Luckily for us, the strategic, being so large, was taking its time to close out its term sheet. So we had time.

Around early September, the founders at Wooplr had started seeing the strategic investment as a constraint and were keen to raise a larger round from a VC. By now, we were quite convinced that taking an alternative approach to fashion commerce in India could be fruitful—fashion was still the hardest nut to crack for e-commerce. The social approach had made the biggest dent in selling online fashion.

We pushed the pedal on our internal approvals and brought the founding team in to present a day before they were supposed to sign the strategic term sheet. We had agreed on the terms beforehand and signed off. Wooplr withdrew its conversations with the strategic on the basis of our promise to give a term sheet soon. These handoffs needed Helion's credibility and a lot of comfort with the founders.

We bought into a company that was still early in proving its business model but was on a very exciting path. It was an alternate path towards building a sticky commerce business around a community without crazy customer acquisition costs.

With financial capital available the way it was in 2014–15, everyone had an inflated sense of how hugely capital-intensive businesses could be funded without flaming out. Even I had mine. In March 2014, my colleague had met a company that was selling software to restaurants to help manage loyalty. Restaurant experience was, at that time, mostly through a walk-in. Food ordering was a small portion of their sales. By June 2014, this company had pivoted to becoming a consumer-side app that would link cashback to the users who ate at a restaurant discovered through the app. The cashback was to be funded by the marketing spend of the restaurant. It had raised angel funding and tested the product in Gurgaon. This company, called CrownIT, was a fully mobile-app-based business. Consumers in Gurgaon had been hearing about this wonderful app that you could 'earn' huge cashback on.

Everyone knew someone who ate out in restaurants all the time and all you needed to do was pick a restaurant recommended by CrownIT. The idea was to tilt a person who wanted to have a Chinese meal to choose Blue Lotus Restaurant, for instance, because it offered a cashback on the customer's spend.

CrownIT had built the app to boost the fill rate of restaurants that had capacity but no predictability. Even popular restaurants wanted more traffic on Mondays because of the uneven load during weekends. Food paired with alcohol provides a massive margin to restaurants. Restaurants were spending 10–15 per cent of their tab on customer acquisition. Five per cent of this marketing spend was going to consumers as a reward and the balance was going to CrownIT.

The founder, Sameer, used to head product at another tech product company and was now balancing the product role with the business role of adding restaurants and thinking of which meal packages to sell to consumers.

We evaluated the business from multiple angles. We spoke to restaurants and their owners. We spoke to customers on what they liked about CrownIT. We also did a deep dive into the product metrics. It was an expensive business to build, but CrownIT could own the online-offline merchant spending business with its early-mover lead. Plus, influencing the spending on restaurants, grocery, local travel and entertainment would add up to billions of dollars. The business had to be built city by city and with Gurgaon and Delhi proven, quickly moving to the Mumbai market would establish a solid lead for CrownIT. The business had to be funded by at least two VCs who could carry the financing load. We crafted our own term sheet and wanted to sign it first before we added the next VC. We had learnt painful lessons from the past when we were ejected out of an investment by the same VC whom we had invited in to partner with us.

Sameer had been talking to Accel also and brought us together on the investment. We jointly invested in CrownIT to help the company establish a presence in Bangalore, Mumbai and Delhi NCR. The plan was to raise a larger round after we had proven financial viability in at least two out of the four cities.

Sales to small and medium businesses like restaurants are not notorious without reason. Collections, to begin with, are a challenge. Restaurants would stall, delay and often refuse to pay the due fees to CrownIT.

We had to serve a wide choice of restaurants. Restaurants that were high on popularity had to be added to the mix. Consumers wanted the ability to earn CrownIT points at these restaurants also and we wanted to help them develop a habit of expecting these points every time they spent at offline businesses. But we had not signed up these 'popular' restaurants so they paid nothing to CrownIT. We offered CrownIT points to users for eating at these 'popular' restaurants from our own pockets.

This meant that for a few months, a few hundred restaurants in every city had to be sent traffic without earning a dime on it.

These two spends were big holes for cash burn at CrownIT. We were prepared for it and expected the cash to last until the next round. CrownIT was a bold business and was bidding for a large outcome. It was dependent on a big financing round, the chances of which looked pretty darn good in late 2014.

Many people mistake any investment by a VC to mean that the VC would make more such investments. In reality, the VC firm is looking to address other themes and is unlikely to make a repeat investment of the same kind. Every investment also forces the VC to shift to what else is out there. So after our investment in Wooplr and CrownIT, our thesis evolved to looking for companies that were massively mass-market purely as a result of a product-market fit. The value proposition had to be so strong that customers would not need to be bribed to use the app. So far, borrowing from the US meant that most of the consumer tech businesses had been targeted at the top bracket of Indian households by income. This income group was the tiny tip of the income pyramid—only 50 million out of 1 billion Indians. Every start-up was targeting the same user with offers, discounts and cashback—and these users were spoilt, fickle and unforgiving.

We wanted massive scale and the common man's needs were the ones that would give us the kind of numbers that we wanted to see.

Travel meant different things to different people. The higher-income-bracket Indians would think of air travel and cabs as the default option. They would start with MakeMyTrip to evaluate options between the cheapest flight options. The next 100 million Indians were connected as well, but thought of buses and trains as their default. RailYatri was a mobile app that predicted delays in train arrivals and the chances of confirmation of waitlisted tickets on trains.

RailYatri came to us via an introduction from a Silicon Valley–based friend who was an angel investor in the company as well as friends with one of the co-founders. Three founders, sitting between Noida, Bangalore and the Bay Area, had raised angel capital and built a product that passengers used during their train journeys. They shared some interesting facts—20 million Indians take long-distance trains every day! The Indian Railways was made up of over twenty-three regional bodies and was not one monolith—information flows were broken and sometimes perverse incentives prevented the sharing of accurate information. Lack of information was a systemic problem.

Travellers were discovering RailYatri from newspaper articles, by word of mouth and through natural search. RailYatri was doing something that was useful. It was providing information that everyone needed. This made all the difference in their user adoption. No free talktime or cashback. The users came and stayed around. In a world where users rarely kept more than two-three apps permanently on their phones, long-distance commuters were choosing to keep the RailYatri app. Usefulness was the third consideration besides memory and data consumption.

We patiently kept track of RailYatri, like we did for many such companies, from May 2014 till December 2014. The trajectory of user acquisition was ramping up steeply. When the founders gave us their fundraise plan, it budgeted that a large proportion of the investment would be used for user acquisition. This was not what we preferred, so I put out a challenge to them—can you grow to 4 million users without spending more than $1 million on it? The founders were candid and referred to their own ask as the 'luxury' ask and my challenge as the more natural path—based on current growth rates, they could grow without burning cash on user acquisition.

From the time we started talking to them to when we invested, the monthly active users at RailYatri had grown from 1,50,000 to 10,00,000. We were really sitting up and paying attention now. A scantily funded start-up had accumulated users at the same rate as others spending $2–3 million to reach the same place. If we continued at the same pace, we would meet my 'challenge' goal. We invested in RailYatri in March 2015. Our main feedback was a suggestion to add more resources to improve the consumer-facing side of the app. When the product team was brought in, they tweaked app discovery and the growth rate improved further.

Out there in the VC world, valuations were still on the rise. This coincided with larger and faster fundraises. Founders now had a sense of 'dilution', which determines how much ownership would be left with them at the end, and they were beginning to understand that raising large rounds of capital was not sustainable if they wanted to retain decent ownership. Investors encouraged large rounds but that caused founder ownership to quickly come down to single digits. VCs have always propagated the notion of the 'bigger pie'—founders can own a large slice of a small pie, but it would be no competition to owning a piece in a bigger pie. The anticipated size of the pie, however, had undergone a scale shift—and large fundraises were necessary to feed growth. But who owned this animal called 'growth'? If the investors owned it, weren't they also responsible for feeding it? If an investor had no ability to put in more capital to keep the fires burning, then was it in the founder's interest to come back to the market for a desperate fundraise? Some founders started questioning the exposure that growth caused for them to the extent that they became insignificant shareholders in their own companies.

In this changing world of growth dominating the funding strategy, founders and investors were now engaged in a tug-of-war between the capital that was needed to fund this growth and ownership of the company.

18

A chat about the 2015 froth would be incomplete without revisiting the incredibly interesting events that unfolded every day at Housing.com. The Housing.com domain had been purchased for $1 million. There were twelve people with co-founder tags. Despite the long list, one name stood out: Rahul Yadav, the CEO and co-founder of Housing.com. Before they raised the big round, they had dazzled the investor community with their data and product approach to solving the real estate discovery problem. It was indeed a beautiful product designed for the consumer. Money had been spent in designing tools to collect real photos from sites. There was talk of drones being used to take aerial shots of the location.

At Helion, we liked the real estate market opportunity. We had, in the process of diligence, tried to assess the persona of Rahul Yadav. He had made it a point to convey his views on the vulnerable businesses built by several well-known entrepreneurs. He lit the fire of his competitiveness by making bold predictions of global dominance directly to the competition. His challenges caught many founders by surprise. They heard him pass judgement on their businesses but didn't have the faintest clue why this young entrepreneur was bothering to call them.

Before we came in, we had a partnership discussion, as always. The founder and business combination was put in the extreme alpha category—it could turn out to be huge or be a bust. It matched the VC expectation of mega outcomes without worrying about the downside. Helion led the second round of investment at Housing. Our investment round came together amidst a lot in investors pushing to get a piece. The company had been built ground-up, like a business that had already achieved its goal of industry domination—employee cost that was at a 30 to 50 per cent premium to the market, a workforce that crossed 1000 in no time, sitting in premium real estate in Mumbai. Softbank invested $100 million in the company. This was one of the largest funding rounds for a company as young as Housing. The already high cash burn went up even further. A very high-decibel nationwide ad campaign was undertaken, which left many consumers intrigued but unsure about what they were supposed to do. Encouraged by the attention from the press, Rahul had emerged as the 'bad boy' of the start-up world. In April 2015, after the final straw in an already rocky board relationship, Rahul quit all his roles related to Housing, but somersaulted by withdrawing his resignation.

Investors can keep a company alive as long as they feel that the person in the driver's seat is not reckless. When so many lives and reputations are involved, responsible action supersedes individual personality, and the board intervened. Not much later, another 'chain-pulling' incident forced the board to take a call. They had to let Rahul go. His presence had become detrimental for the business.[4]

In his brief time in the sun, Rahul rocked the investor–founder relationship so hard that the traditional pattern of dependency in the relationship had been shattered. How long can a VC board wait for the founder CEO to pay heed to advice and guidance? If he tells his board that he does not find their advice helpful, how can a VC board continue to engage? For everyone associated with Housing.com, Rahul taught valuable lessons.[5]

I joined the board of Housing.com after Rahul Yadav quit and made an announcement that he would distribute his shares to employees. I missed the action that had made Rahul famous. Jason, an entrepreneur from the US who had turned around a loss-making business and sold it profitably just after graduating, had been brought in as CEO. From my joining the board to the eventual merger of the business with PropTiger, Jason's days would be spent cutting costs, trimming the workforce and generating sales. He also had to deal with the dynamics of having three investors, one of whom was the big daddy, SoftBank.

It was a serious exercise, bringing back the culture of productive action. It would seem routine from the outside, but a company that had so many unproductive parts needed a lot of axle grease to move it forward with the new discipline of cash conservation. The Housing.com saga would always be remembered as one that set a new benchmark for pissing off the greatest number of people in the least possible time.

Housing.com left a much-needed sobering message about how even $120 million funding is sometimes not enough to fund hubris that flies above reason.

As a VC in Silicon Valley in 2000, I saw the dominoes fall in slow motion. The signs were similar—heightened optimism driving risk taking and capital overflow from the least likely places, causing irrational valuation. The low cost of entrepreneurship made it mandatory to become an entrepreneur or suffer the torturous 'fear of missing out' or FOMO. Start-ups were stuck with ten-year leases that they couldn't get out of, employee stock options that were worthless and layoffs in the thousands. A carpet-store owner who sold very expensive rugs on University Avenue in downtown Palo Alto became a prolific angel and actually did better on his investments than many VCs who had to shut shop after 2001. By the summer of 2015, I was already telling the founders of companies whose boards I was on to start planning for a slowdown in funding. I had seen enough quick failures and expensive flameouts to know that this was coming.

In Gurgaon, I had neighbours coming by to take advice on the start-up ideas they'd had the previous night at the pub or a start-up investment idea that they were recommended to invest in. The fever was spreading.

Many start-ups spent a lot of time dressing up for the big round, and when it was finally done they had no idea what to do with the money in the bank. In the heat of the battle for raising capital, sometimes the very purpose of the capital would get lost. As VCs, we sometimes had to remind founders that our capital would make the biggest impact if it could be spent in a framework designed to provide the maximum lift in performance. For this, the start-up had to throw out its 'old engine' and design a new, zippier one for the journey ahead. The new engine would yield more bang for the buck and take the start-up on a steeper trajectory. We did this fit-out through a ninety-day plan that we designed with founders even before the legal agreements of the new funding were complete. It was not easy to identify the gaps that needed to be addressed immediately, but after much convincing that as investors we wouldn't run away on learning about the holes in the business, founders usually opened up. The common goal was not to waste time figuring out which holes to fill once the money clock started. Every day was precious once the money hit. That's why I used to be particularly frustrated when legal debate between us and the founder would delay the company from moving—speed and timing were all-important.

In the ninety-day plan, we determined the open positions, gave out the job search mandates, identified the relevant metrics and also determined the 'guard rails' within which we had to remain and not drift too far from when pushing the pedal, like customer stickiness. If they started losing it at the cost of growth, then we had to pull back and fix the drift before pushing forward again. The ninety-day plan helped us tremendously in setting the company off on a good trajectory.

The culture of 'grow big or go home' was taking root. Powai, the home of IIT Bombay, was a fertile belt for high-growth start-ups.[6] Some people claim that the culture at IIT Bombay was conducive for producing founders who had the chutzpah for high-growth execution.

TinyOwl, a Powai-based food delivery start-up, was servicing local food orders at the time of its first VC round. One of its first big spends was on a fancy office in the same business park as Housing.com.[7] It raised $20 million in quick funding rounds and tried to rush through a culture of becoming a big company in a hurry. I would hear about people who would collect offer letters at an off-market salary from Housing.com and then go over to TinyOwl to get an even more preposterous offer.

Both TinyOwl and Housing got fancy offices too early in their lifecycles. Both companies burnt cash like there was no end to its supply. Both laid off employees in the hundreds. The TinyOwl layoff was the low point of this frothy period—young founders making wrong choices, young employees having their start-up dreams cut short by layoffs, and anger all around. After TinyOwl, I didn't have to waste my breath prophesizing the cash crunch period. Every founder had turned sober and was figuring out how to survive. The party was over.

19

There were two kinds of founders at the end of 2015—the ones who had already burnt all the cash they had raised and the ones who had some dry powder left. The ones who burnt through the capital ranged from those who exhausted $1–3 million to those who spent $100 million with nothing to show for it. You had to be either lucky or conservative if you were in the second category.

Success had been equated with growth. Growth meant that you had to ignore some basic questions about sustainability. When I sat in the board meeting of a start-up I had no clue about my own position on this sensitive topic—the peer pressure was so great that it sounded insincere to talk about conserving cash. I would feel two-faced asking about the growth rate and then ending the meeting with concerns about the insufficient amount of capital left.

We had learnt to become metric-oriented—every presentation would contain more and more data. But it was hard to guess what was meaningful and what was plain vanity. Over time, we learnt that while we started out driving gross-level growth, we had to switch to identifying the relevant metric as the business grew.

CrownIT, the restaurant rewards app, was dependent on a large financing round. By mid-2015, the cash was beginning to dry up. A high cash-burn business could sense the breeze and rethink its plan, slow the burn but keep the same goal. Hoping that we could eventually raise a large round to fund our plans, we put the brakes on a lot of the business parts that seemed unnecessary. Whatever was not important in the next six months had to be dropped.

People had to be let go of. I was less conflicted. I was pushing for the discovery of organic growth channels that did not cost as much as paying every user. The product went through a redesign, and a slower accumulation of cashback replaced direct, simple cashback on every purchase. The hit on cash was delinked slightly from user growth. We slowed the growth and tapered off the burn to extend the runway. The board dialogue was now a very honest revisit to product market fit. It was like going back to the drawing board. The cost basis for the business was at minimum fat content. This meant that all unnecessary spend had to be brutally slashed. The company had to only feed muscles which were essential for the business.

Many start-ups were having similar discussions with their investors at that point. CrownIT was lucky to have a founder who didn't want to give up and investors who were in for the long haul. Many other start-ups which had small investments from a club of investors were not as lucky. In a club setting, no one stepped forward to decide about the future.

The financing environment went from bad to worse and we had to eventually rethink our original ambitious target of becoming the online app for offline spends. If we had raised another $20 million round, we could have carried on, but as long as the profitability of the business was unclear, we would not know whether we had scale for scale's sake or were building a real business. That point was somewhere in the distant future.

The word 'pivot' became popular among start-ups in mid-2015. Start-ups that had some capital left could keep going down the unsustainable path till they hit a wall. We had honest conversations with most of our founders about what the end could look like. The tough ask here was to come up with a more sustainable business, prove that it had some legs, and come back to the market to raise smaller rounds. The immediate question was, how long do we continue the façade? Or do we bite the bullet and drop the facade? In the midst of all this, there were also some companies that had figured out growth and had high stickiness of users but did not have a revenue model. A less negative funding environment would have been more forgiving. But in 2015, the road stretched very far ahead, and not having a revenue model meant there was no chance in hell of raising investor capital.

Online marketplaces for home services was another prematurely overfunded sector by 2015. There was a clutter of companies providing vertical services like home painting or tuition services and some horizontal ones like UrbanClap.

Tiger invested $5 million in a company called LocalOye. With an investor that had the capability of writing a large cheque for subsequent rounds, LocalOye's funding had raised the ante on capital burn in the space. SAIF and Accel had invested $1.5 million in UrbanClap. We thought the race was still open and wanted to throw one more company into the mix. We invested in an open marketplace for home services called Doormint. The team was serving the Powai area in Mumbai.

The investment amount was not miserly and was shared with another VC firm. The funding was large enough to prove the business and allow the company to comfortably raise the next round. Home services was the last major category that was funded before the gates closed in late 2015.

Doormint couldn't make it through to the other side. They squeezed their burn and realized that the home services business was not possible to deliver on without raising large buckets of cash. The founders were amazing in trying the pivot route—instead of focusing on a horizontal, they chose to focus on the laundry vertical. The pivot was run like a machine. They made an effort to turn the entire laundry operation into a process. The finding was that laundry was not amenable to tech enablement and costs added up the moment you tried to go beyond local markets. The minimum price that had to be charged to wash one piece of clothing was so high that the service could never become compelling to the masses. This would limit the market size. After an intense effort to figure out the pivot, the founders concluded that its scalability and cash requirement made it unfeasible. It was the display of an A-grade team stuck in a C-grade market.

By 2016, VCs hit the pause button on investments. The small cheques that helped new companies get off the ground had all but disappeared. A few mega rounds had kept the clock turning on total capital invested, but that impacted just a handful of companies. The majority were starving or quietly shutting down.

VCs had a cartload of young start-ups that they had signed seed cheques to—these were reviewed. In a tightening funding environment, the portfolio adds from 2014 and 2015 were the first priority for each VC. Almost all of them were candidates for an internal bridge round. Every VC made sure that their own companies had cash and stopped investing in new companies.

The years 2014 and 2015 were seminal for VCs. They were the coming-of-age years for VC firms and the people who worked in them. The business of VC had been reduced to investing and picking the right company. The competitiveness among VC firms also increased in 2014. Not for just winning the deals, but also for who we were. Who was better, stronger, faster. Good deals in a geographical market like India are also a zero-sum game. Like our start-ups winning their markets, the best start-ups are not evenly distributed among all VCs.

As it often happens in India, employees at VC firms began to actively compare among themselves. Compensation data got shared across firms. Dissonance was rising. The first frothy cycle of Indian venture capital had tested us on the long-term view of the business. We all seemed to be hunting, hustling and closing new investments—and to the outside world it seemed that was enough: enough to build firms and provide stable VC platforms for institutional investors. It wasn't.

The onus of not missing the Paytms and BookMyShows of this generation was on the VCs. Founders were now savvy and making smart choices. They asked questions of their VCs. Did the VC partner understand their space? Where did they have a relationship? Who could help them raise bigger rounds in future?

Hunting and winning were a large part of the business. If the teams were not out there talking to founders at cafes and bars and signing term sheets in their apartments, deals would be lost for good. Funds were becoming larger and partners had let go of decision-making in favour of the younger investment team. This had less to do with long-term succession planning and more to do with competition.

VC firms in India were set up to make centralized decisions with hunting delegated to the junior team members. Decision-making was a series of discussions that picked unique aspects of the start-up, and the past learnings of the firm were then applied to the new situation. Always a frustrating exercise for the investment team that felt excited about the start-up and then had to be subjected to a bunch of questions by a team that looked at the deal a lot more cynically. The disconnects were mostly around the highly subjective topic of founders' ability to build a scale business.

This would slow down the process and some other firm with a higher degree of delegation or money-losing ability would walk away with the deal.

Froth in the investment environment had sharply tilted the deliverables of the VC business to the teams that had the first contact with the founders. These teams were expected to react quickly on 'deals with buzz' and prevent hierarchical decision-making. The reshaped expectations of the market were that 'great' founders had to be hunted and firms had to minimize the number of touchpoints that founders had to go through before a decision.

At Helion, our investment team was mature and experienced. The new partners had been hired as VPs with at least eight years of work experience. Two of them had been promoted to partner roles in 2015 and one had joined laterally as a partner from an operating role.

The way we had structured the investment team was that a team of three was attached to each theme—this tag team would decide which investments to bring up to the partnership. The three team members would include a founding partner, one of the freshly graduated partners, and one of the analysts who would assist them.

This arrangement was helping us move fast and the tag teams were self-imposing a high bar on investments that came up. In such a gated process, the quality of most deals that came up for group review had to be kept high, so there was an implicit affirmation from the team that proposed the investment. Being theme-oriented, the tag teams were domain experts and that trust meant they knew best which deals had to be recommended for approval.

We invested in eleven new start-ups in 2014 and eleven more in 2015. These were our most prolific years as a VC firm.

We were finally a firm with a smooth rhythm—single-minded, focused and an execution engine. The portfolio was adding up quickly and we were proud of all the investments we made. Making a departure from our image as an over-thoughtful firm, we took bold bets, which, in the past, would have died a natural death under the weight of over-deliberation. We were never weak on taking opportunistic left-field calls. We invested in some unusual start-ups: a beauty salon company, for example! So we couldn't have been faulted for being traditional in our thinking. In the new world, a CrownIT was a bold investment. Housing.com was an all or nothing. That was an example of an investment that VCs ought to be doing—it would most likely have an extreme outcome, which means it would either lead to nothing or give a return that equalled the profit from the entire fund.

In 2015, with eleven investments completed, we had to do a budgeting exercise. How much more capital would the Fund Three portfolio need until the exit? The math required a future view on capital that a company would need to raise, and based on our ownership, how much our share of that capital would turn out to be. We applied some probability on timing and success for each company.

The final number was close to the total investible capital that was left over from the third fund. So effectively, we were done with Fund Three. This meant that we would need to hit the road pretty soon. Fund Four had to be raised. Our investors were based all over the world and talking to all of them required a long lead time. The financial world had again gone into wait-and-watch mode—their investments were now illiquid for longer periods. More late-stage capital helped keep venture-funded companies stay private for longer periods of time. Pressure to list had been replaced by the notion that 'We can remain private and keep growing because there is more private capital available'. No one was getting an exit. One of the well-regarded institutional investors we met in New York told us wryly that 'in a way, the return in the dotcom crash was better than now, because at least companies were going public in 2000'. Perception of venture had become more illiquid than before.

We were in the ninth year of operations and our total capital under management was $650 million. We had come a long way from our first fund. Back then, we were just another first-time fund. Now, we were a top-tier firm in the hottest asset class in the fastest-growing market in the world. Our investors drew comfort from VC firms that were being built for the long term. We were designed like a platform. Our HR practices, financial controls and three funds under management were all in a good place.

On our way to achieving our original vision of being a founder-centric firm, we had built a reputation of trust and our operating heavy model was scaling up well—helping start-ups with strategic HR, recruitment, product and financial management. Our team was culturally cohesive—it was carrying on the values that we had set for the firm, like humility, respect and value addition.

But the dynamics of the ever-changing set of market opportunities and a firm's ability to outperform its peers in every cycle makes it one of the most exciting businesses to be in. That's why icons fall by the wayside and new titans emerge.

Every VC firm has its peculiarities. It is very hard to look at them from the outside and figure out what is really happening. Any definite description of a VC firm would be outdated by the time it was written. Its core, though, remains the same: a diverse mix of people interacting with each other and the market and taking investment calls with half-baked information. The longer they do it, the more they know what does not work. With some luck, they also know what does work. The 'wisdom' and 'culture' acquired over time become the bedrock for the future.

Despite past successes, an existential discontinuity emerges sooner or later for every VC firm.

Teams need to transition. As Lord Tennyson wrote, 'The old order changeth, yielding place to new.' As new technology cycles emerge, time after time, as the attractive opportunities of the past give way to new ones, the old guard needs to let go and let a new sheriff run the town.

In a VC firm, highly intellectual people get together to perform non-management roles without traditional business metrics like sales performance and profitability to guide hierarchy definition. Most people join VC firms as mentees and learn the ropes while making expensive mistakes. Mentors guide thinking. With no real organizational structure, the dynamics of leadership are driven by this loose relationship of mentor and mentee.

Over time, mentees expect to graduate and take their seats next to their mentors. The younger investment partners carry forward the firm's DNA, build a stronger brand and continue the good work. Economics are passed down from older partners to new partners because the value will be created by the younger lot. When your profession has the word 'capitalist' in it, the cold hard logic around economic incentives can't be ignored. Otherwise the business would be called Venture and Sons.

This graduation is usually co-timed with a successful investment hit where the mentee has played an important role and proven their value to the firm. In VC firms, successful outcomes are few and sometimes hailed prematurely. Graduation gets you to participate in the full economics of profits-sharing in an equitable manner.

In the absence of a specific graduation date, these transitions become hard to time. Some firms, like Benchmark, only hire partners so the whole qualitative call on graduation is not thrust upon them.

Unless there has been a bumper crop of successes, it's unlikely that the graduation will occur for more than one mentee.

In the process of graduation, the mentors do not become redundant—their ability to charter the course for the next ten-twenty years for the firm has only gotten stronger. They know what institutional investors are thinking, where the world is going, the elements that have driven success, and how the firm should make strategic choices. With bigger, newer entrants in the tech investing world, challenges for VC firms are only growing and the keepers of the 'old wisdom' can keep the firm future-proof.

Being a co-founder, I thought of myself as part of the firm I was building. I had more than a job. It was bigger than that. In my head, I was Helion. I had dreamt of it in 2004 and now it stood around me in flesh and blood.

Around the time we were starting our investor conversations, our investment team was feeling unsettled about the future. The intense competition between firms had been driving up self-introspection in the team. Decision-making seemed more hierarchical than in other firms. The other guys seemed more motivated and better compensated.

The future was uneven, and in the middle of the new fund conversations, there had been no internal discussions on reorganizing the team. The team wanted a change. The firm was having the most important strategic HR review in its history. The tremors had reached a crescendo and decisions had to be taken. Mentees wanted to graduate. Now. Before the new fund.

For two-three months, the teams went back and forth on options. When the internal discussions came to pass, the new partners presented a proposal to equalize every partner, old and new, on economics and how the firm should be run. This proposal was a possible solution but no agreement was reached and it was decided that the three new partners would leave the firm. They planned to start a firm on their own. It was a painful outcome for me. I had decided to stay with the firm I had helped create. 31 December 2015 was the last day at work for two of the three partners and 1 March 2016 was the last day for the third. These departures were a big blow to the firm, which had been brought to a crossroads.

A team departure of this magnitude raised a question mark on the firm—only three investment professionals were left from the original team of seven. The institutional investors were hugely disappointed with the outcome.

When you lose a top-tier platform after nine years of building it, its repercussions are felt amongst its sixty-odd investments, its investors and the entrepreneur community. The press loved the intrigue and the fall story and some 'friends' thoughtfully forwarded me articles about it. Just in case I had missed them. Our colleagues in other VC firms were distressed to see us disband and called to offer help.

The good news in all this was that the decision was clean and fast. We did not live in animosity just to keep a business alive. It would not have been fair to our investors. Our founders were looking for clarity, and the steps that followed were to assure every company that Helion as a firm would stand behind them as before. A few responsibilities were reassigned to manage continuity. Our investors all had questions and we answered each of them in as detailed a manner as possible.

I decided to stay back, and for the following year, we all put our noses to the grindstone to make sure the stability in our portfolio was back. Helion decided not to raise any fresh funds, and the remaining partners continued to manage the portfolio. A good story ended abruptly and we lost the potential to build a firm that outlived us.

20

Stability was the need of the hour. My days were now spent taking stock of the portfolio companies. I continued to go to the Gurgaon office. The Aravalis had been consumed a little more by greed from the time we had moved into our office in Vatika Towers, with several new condominiums sprouting out from behind the keekars. Golf Course Road, where we were located, had started getting dug up for the Rapid Metro project. Many more restaurants had sprung up from when we had first moved in. There was a little cafe serving instant coffee and Maggi on the ground floor of the building. My commute had switched to online cabs. Sometimes I would not have the exact cash to pay the cab fare and end up ordering instant coffee just to pay the fare. I was distracted and concentrating on the road would have been hard in any case. The roads were fuller and the traffic crazier. I had no desire to drive myself into a tractor.

Getting to office every day for the past ten years had always been a soothing experience after the melee on the roads. Our new office, into which we had moved only two years back, was an island of calm. There was hardly any noise and everything was spotless. Tastefully fitted out with expensive furniture, the look reflected just how long-term the plan was while designing it. Most visitors would comment on two things—the quiet and the tidiness. But now it was quieter than planned. In the last year or so, our analysts and junior staff had moved on to other jobs. My assistant, Lilian, who had brought so much productivity into my life by putting my entire life on the calendar, was also moving on. The office felt very empty—for the last several years, every time I entered, I would first meet my associate. I would always expect to see him hunched over his laptop, staring at an Excel model. He was no longer around. By the middle of 2016, our CFO, Nats, had also moved on. We had shut down our Bangalore office and consolidated everything in the Gurgaon office.

We had stopped looking at fresh investments, but I kept receiving emails asking me to look at new opportunities. Most people did not understand what had just happened. Some would ask me, has Helion shut down? It was the wrong question. VC firms don't shut down until you sell every company on the balance sheet and return the capital to the investors. No, we had not shut down. What is a VC firm that is not making any new investments? Not having cash at all times to invest in new companies is not an exceptional event. It happens if there are gaps between raising funds. This time we were not going to raise another fund. Our balance capital would go to the companies we had already invested in. So, as an active investor, Helion's days were done.

When I look back at the Helion journey, I see it as a journey of evolution. The timing didn't work out in the end, but we started the firm with good intentions and did reasonably well establishing our name and making good investments.

The core value in a VC firm is a competency I would call the 'deal-selection muscle'. Born out of the unique DNA of each firm, this muscle is a complex network of openness to recognize past mistakes, having people around to institutionalize the lessons from these mistakes and carrying the gumption of investing in deals that might make you look stupid. Some of the worst investments we made were the ones on which we had all agreed heartily.

The deal-selection muscle had to be worked on and used over and over again.

Our second fund chose to diversify on an axis that we thought would be a common underpinning to our thesis. At the firm, the investment partners diverged in their thinking because our investment areas were so far apart from each other. The commonality we expected was missing and the strengthening of the deal-selection muscle was compromised. We did a deep dive into many verticals like travel, financial services, education and health.

Our second fund diversification was not successful, but it put us in a good place to look at all these areas with the common underpinning of how consumer Internet would disrupt them. By the third fund, the team was working on thesis areas that tied back to each other—my mobility thesis tied back to online retail, the offline-online thesis tied back to verticals like restaurants and food delivery, education to ed tech.

Focusing our energies into defined themes helped our third fund pick many winners.

What was gone with the departed team at Helion was the learning that had been gained by evaluating at least 5000 start-ups in the past ten years, the value of the team that had established a system of finding the right companies, investigating them closely and then making a complex decision based on facts, joint imagination and past experience. The goodwill we had earned with our investors was lost. Their expectation of backing a stable firm that would last a long time had been dashed. The uncomfortable questions on what happened would linger. For all of us.

Like all unexpected shocks, over time, what is initially unreal slowly gets internalized and accepted. Reality sets in and the past looks distant.

My coffee would often go cold as I stared out of my window at the new Rapid Metro line being constructed along Golf Course Road. My mind drifted between the past and the future. Where was I headed? What would I like to do next? I was in two minds. I had spent a decade working on building Helion. My portfolio was doing well and I had insights on what worked and what didn't work in India. Helion investors wanted me to commit time to the fund and continue to manage my portfolio. It was more than fair for them to ask for this. The investments were new and needed time to mature and build a solid foundation for growth.

Do I go back to putting together a new fund? Usually, the first fund is small as investors expect the manager to prove their adherence to thesis and ability to put together a quality team. There is the effort of putting together a team, establishing a high-intensity but intellectually honest culture. The constant tug-of-war with the portfolio founders. The midnight calls. The emotional investment into other people's success. The running around the world to meet investors. And all this could come to naught unless the fund was wildly successful. I had heard stories of people raising new funds having to constantly be on the road. It would take at least twelve months, maybe twenty-four. People grimly talked about making 300 pitches and still not being done raising their fund. I had spent most of my time with start-ups, not with investors. I had to build my relationships and relearn the whole process of pitching to prospective investors. At a time when India was not at all on the minds of global investors! The investors who had already invested in India over the last ten years were waiting to see exits. Even Flipkart, which seemed the most promising, had still not given any returns to investors. How did one identify investors who had not yet invested in an India fund but were open to the idea? They could be in any country, on any continent. To find them, I would have to boil the ocean. It would require hearing a hundred 'nos' for every 'yes'. Was my brain capable of handling the rejection? Was my ego going to survive the brutal rejection?

Or do I do nothing?

I had to decide soon.

I was not doing well dealing with this uncertainty. The stress had started causing me to lose a lot of weight. Everyone I met would remark on my 'fitness', whereas the real reason was just stress-induced weight loss. I had to repeatedly reassure my worried mother that I was eating as much as before. Months dragged on with this uncertainty.

21

I had now been a VC for twenty years. Starting off at twenty-six years of age as the first employee at Walden International's India fund in 1998, I had seen three cycles of boom and bust as a VC.

The last few years had been devoted to finding start-ups and investing in them. The older ones were maturing and the young ones were figuring it out. They had gone through their own journeys. Making mistakes, learning, flaming out, dying, experiencing rebirth, but not stagnating.

By early 2017, we had completed a year of stabilization at Helion. UnitedLex had crossed $100 million in revenue in 2016. After many years of breakneck growth, it was now slowing down to a more reasonable 20 to 30 per cent per year. The team was still led by Dan as CEO. The operations had grown a lot more extensively in the US than Gurgaon. So, contrary to our belief, UnitedLex became a legal services company without offshoring much business to India. At this time, it was one of the top three companies in the legal outsourcing space and was considered to be an industry leader. We had gone from zero revenue to market leadership. UnitedLex had appeared on the radar of potential acquirers several times. We had now started paying attention to these conversations. As the largest shareholders, we did not want to rock the boat, but still had to look out for our own exit.

Vasu, the CEO at Equitas, the microfinance company, was very aware of the challenges that had surrounded the sector in the form of regulatory pressure and overcrowding. Although his business came out of the Andhra Pradesh crisis almost unscathed, there was a clear takeaway for Vasu from the event. Andhra Pradesh could happen again, in a new state. The politico-social crossfire was inescapable. Reacting to this risk, Vasu and his team had diversified the business into many more lines, with a second business engine now revving up in the used-vehicle finance space. The founding team had come together from a background in vehicle finance, and they took to building the used-vehicle business like pros. The company had been approved to act like a small finance bank. It could now open accounts for the long queues of Indians who were too small to be served by traditional banks.

Vasu had committed to his investors that 2016 would be the year for the IPO. True to Vasu's style, he took the date seriously even when some of his investors had forgotten. Work started like clockwork a year in advance. Bankers were appointed and all the investors were engaged. For an investor,

IPO preparation ranks very high on the list of 'most pleasurable things to do'.

We had to commit to selling a part of our ownership to meet the criterion for minimum offer for sale. Equitas went public in April 2016 on the National Stock Exchange, raising over Rs 2000 crore.

Spandana, the microfinance company, managed to keep generating a profit all these years and repaying its banker syndicate. Padmaja still ran the business. She had not lost her focus or energy. Although Spandana lost a few senior leaders who had been vital during the crisis, it rebuilt its leadership team. The RBI remained a big supporter to the battered sector throughout the crisis. The larger microfinance companies were allowed to become small finance banks. Spandana was still choked by a balance sheet because of the hole it had to first fill. They were not allowed to borrow more till they had repaid the loans taken from banks before the crisis.

A large Indian PE firm entered the scene and decided to go through the trouble of cleaning up the balance sheet and funding the company afresh. This transaction required infinite forbearance. Each bank was deciding its course of action on its own. The PE firm's offer to buy them all out had to be agreed to by all twenty-two banks. Talk about herding cats. With everyone on their last ounce of strength, the last bank signed off. The six-year-old lock on growth was finally opened and Spandana started life anew with $100 million in fresh funding.

Shubham had grown well and taken a leadership position in the micro-housing market while keeping its mission intact. It had grown to eighty locations across India and now employed more than 1000 people. Sanjay and Ajay had provided steady hands at growth. The company had raised three rounds of capital by 2016, with its last round coming from a PE investor. More competitors had jumped in to take a piece of the mega market, but the growth had given everyone enough room to space out the market.

We had exchanged our LetsBuy shares for Flipkart shares in 2012. This flip had done well for us. We sold our Flipkart holding at a decent value and generated a high multiple on our cost.

Seclore, the data protection company functioning out of Mumbai, had successfully grown to markets outside India and now had an office in Sunnyvale, CA, which the CEO, Vishal, operated out of. It had added several large customers in Europe and the US. A team had been hired to manage US sales and marketing.

RailYatri had been racking up its monthly active users and reached a monthly user base of ten million. It crossed the four million user goal six months ahead of schedule. They integrated a food delivery business for customers travelling by train. This transactional business was the first service offered to the massive base of active customers using RailYatri. We could see it steadily climbing the ranks of the most downloaded apps for travel. With one revenue stream locked, they were now figuring out bus and train tickets.

MoEngage, the marketing automation company, had progressed steadily, adding customers, including most of the top unicorns in India. It had made a strong entry in South East Asia by selling to the local unicorns. Large enterprise customers like global telecom leaders were beginning to evaluate MoEngage's unique mobile-first approach. Ravi was maturing well as a strong CEO. He combined the engineering strength that was in the MoEngage DNA with a customer-centric view.

Two years after we funded Wooplr, it went from being a social network for fashion that indirectly influenced fashion commerce to a transaction business that relied on influencers to generate sales. It took a bold bet to shut down its own e-commerce business and turned 100 per cent into a business that enabled social influencers to sell merchandise. From its original learning on keeping customer acquisition costs low, the company was trying to build capital-efficient social commerce.

CrownIT, the app for offline commerce space and the last investment from the Helion fund, had pivoted. Its customers were now no longer restaurants. Its ability to motivate people to answer questions was redirected to seek answers on behalf of brands, which then used this knowledge to make decisions about their brand positioning and promotion. The burn was no longer at the crazy levels it used to be and there was enough cash in the bank to keep building better research tools.

The portfolio was looking strong. The companies had by and large made amends on time. Running out of money was not a scenario we were worried about in any of them. The founders had figured it out.

In the last one year, I had pulled back from the day-to-day activity of meeting new start-ups and used the time to evaluate the long-term trajectory of India's venture business. There was a lot going on. The VC industry was growing. Funds had become bigger in size. A new set of associates and VPs with connections to their college peer founders had joined VC firms. In a way, the sector was going through a rebirth and freshness was coming in. New lessons, new investors and new role models. VC firms were now truly institutionalizing themselves. The large ones were spending a lot of effort on marketing their value-add.

While Helion was out of the game for new investments, after a lull in venture investments in 2015, by 2016, the activity in the start-up world had picked up again. Other VC firms had also cleaned up their portfolios and were back to active investing. These last four years had been crazy but a necessary stepping stone to the future. The start-up culture was now well-established. For the VCs, the founders who had survived 2015 were those who had taken the hard knocks and gone through a period of heavy learning. They looked even more credible to back. These founders were demanding of their VCs. They wanted to partner with VCs who could provide depth in thinking and strategy inputs specific to the industry vertical that the start-ups belonged to.

After the copycat business model phase, start-ups targeted India-specific problems. These problems had existed for decades but there were now new ways of looking at them. A generation that had grown as technology consumers did not see problems in the same way as the generation of technology builders who came before them. They could now see a technology product at the centre of the solution. The new telecom provider, Jio, had been allowing users to access the Internet at prices lower than ever. Start-ups were beginning to see their user bases grow more painlessly than before, when it cost a lot of marketing spend to acquire new users. Language had broken barriers alongside the growing pervasiveness of data connectivity. Start-ups were taking into account users who were more comfortable in regional languages than in English.

India's VC opportunity had started off neck-and-neck with China's, but in the last decade, had been left behind. The fact was that there had been little to show in terms of large exits. India had still to prove its worth as a destination to make exciting financial returns for investors in VC firms. As an insider, I knew that there were now many strong contenders in the wings compared to five years back. There was many a slip between the cup and the lip in VCs selling their winners and returning capital to their investors. Like a very experienced PE investor once told me, returns on private investments mean nothing until you heard the money in your pocket.

I was not looking for a job. I had to decide whether I should take on the humungous task of restarting my journey to create a new VC fund. It would be taxing and long. Starting a VC fund was not at all like starting a company. It was asking an investor to write you a cheque with no idea of where the money would be used. The complexity increased manifold between investing as an angel in a start-up and running a VC firm that has to 'manage capital' over a decade. The first and foremost task was to build a partnership that could operate around a structure that would gradually evolve to suit individual needs, yet not be so loose that the firm was effectively a collection of independent investment people coming together. Venture capital was a team sport with individual responsibility. Our team had to build the 'decision muscle' and hone it with every cheque we wrote. It was a long path and I had to be clear that I wanted to walk it.

There were many questions in my head and I had to seek the answers before the year ended.

In the last twelve years, I had followed a thesis and put together a portfolio that had a high exit rate. For investments made in the slow environment of the last decade, this was an uncommon outcome. My investments were in companies that were attractive to others to buy out or list publicly. I had proven to myself that I could, on average, pick and help build a decent number of companies that were of value to someone. Investing and harvesting are the two sides of the VC business and need to be achieved in conjunction. One cannot be successful without the other. We did not plan it that way, but of our investments, those that were focused on the greater mass of consumers who were not in the top income bracket were the ones that scaled best. Equitas had a successful IPO. Even the big bet on Spandana didn't completely disappoint, with it preparing for an IPO in 2019. Shubham Housing also had a high likelihood of listing in the public market. These were businesses focused on serving middle India.

My basket of mistakes was heavy after having actively invested for the last twelve years. Some of the mistakes had changed my investment approach. Until BookMyShow, I used to rely on Excel models to understand market size. The results were usually uninspiring, leading to a rejection of the start-up due to market size. Now I knew better than to base my thinking only on market size. As long as there was an inherent ability to grow non-linearly, India's teeming masses would always provide limitless demand. I never factored in the capital needs of a business and the potential threat to a business that burns at life-threatening levels. Assessing founder quality now carried a hundred nuances for me. I had taken journeys with the brightest of them, which only a few fortunate individuals have the pleasure of experiencing. I had seen the best times and the worst times for these entrepreneurs. The interesting bit was that nine out of ten were not perfect. They all had serious handicaps, but which handicap could be ignored for which journey was the key to the decision. Sometimes the handicap had a solution and sometimes it was a fatal flaw.

I had participated in hundreds of decisions that our firm took on investing capital. Looking back, there was a pattern to how we made good decisions and how, sometimes, with the same level of information, we got it wrong. I also had a fairly good idea of the company building process—I now had a good practical sense for sequencing vital activities in the early part of a start-up's journey that could save precious time and capital. I learnt to have a priority item about each start-up that, according to me, was the most important issue to address at that point—to put this on an agenda with the founder-CEO through discussion and data. This honed my interaction from just taking inputs and reacting to founder-CEOs during board meetings to having a point of view. I also learnt to periodically ask myself a simple question about the start-ups I had invested in—would I put all the capital at my disposal into this company if I could? Why not? Or why?

Many start-ups refused to die or get bought out—they just hung around as an investment on the VC's balance sheet. I had even seen the pain of getting rid of these 'initially exciting investments' off the VC fund's balance sheets. So, in one eye I could wear the pragmatic lens and in the other the optimistic lens.

I was also excited about some new tools that were beginning to be used to make better investment decisions. From my VC friends in the US, I began to learn and appreciate the power of data science to help drive growth in these businesses. From Twitter to Facebook to Slack, data science has come a long way in helping us understand and predict how customers are behaving. Data science was now being used to assess the quality of customer traction and predict how well the product was adopted by customers.

I concluded my thinking. I wanted to build a new VC firm from scratch. Even after a decade, there was an opportunity to build a VC firm that would participate in the success of the new crop of start-ups. India had evolved and the VC business needed to break the old mould. I was standing at an important juncture, where the old chapter was ending and a new one was beginning. With my ability to learn from the past and with an eye on the future, I could help craft a new-age VC firm that would resonate with founders.

I spoke to my wife about my options. After so many years of prioritizing Helion over the family, I owed it to her. Any decision I would take would affect my family—it was no longer about career advancement. It needed to be aligned with the family's needs. Her buy-in was important for me because I would need to excuse myself from most responsibilities at home over the next few years. She was glad that I had decided on a path instead of being miserable. She knew a bit about the odds, but the only thing she said was that I should do it. She tried her best not to ask any questions that would seem like she had doubts. I knew this would be the pillar I needed at this time. She would have to be a single parent for some more time and postpone any plans for cosy family vacations.

The situation was too complicated to explain to my parents. They had been super proud of Helion. I was not sure if they knew what had happened. I tried to explain one night over the phone, but didn't hear any response. Not entirely sure if they had understood, I ended the call. One day, my father called me and gave me his blessings to restart the journey. He had understood where things stood and what path I was planning to take.

Before starting the marathon fundraise, we took a short break in Goa with a friend and his family. When he heard about the plan from my wife, he immediately asked, 'So what's Plan B?' As emphatically as she could, she replied, 'There is no Plan B.' I thanked heaven that day for the support I had from my family for my dream and also felt a little scared about the risk I was going to take.

There had been too much noise about Helion. While I was not entirely ready, I decided to announce my own plans as distinct from the firm. I picked a date and made a press release. The media reception was generous. As if there was no pressure already, with my grand announcement of raising a new fund, I had made it worse. I chose the name Unitary Helion for the new fund. I picked Unitary as a name because it meant 'forming a single, unified entity'. It would be good to build a firm that followed this principle. I retained Helion in the name because somewhere in my heart I believed that the name still had a strong resonance with founders.

It was now October 2017. I had spent the last month preparing a rough pitch deck and lining up meetings with as many institutional investors as I could. These meetings would need a month to cover. I would have to travel to London, Zurich, Amsterdam in Europe; in the US, the West Coast, Texas, Pittsburgh, New York; and Abu Dhabi. My main goal was to cover as much ground as I could to make the broad outreach and set up first meetings with investors while the pieces for putting the fund together fell into place.

It was 11 p.m., and I had to start my journey. The kids were asleep in their beds. I had given them goodnight hugs with a long, tight squeeze. It was a strange moment. They had not seen me in this frame of mind. I was relieved, worried and optimistic at the same time. Perhaps the kids felt these emotions too, and I got a long squeeze back in return. They were growing up.

My wife saw me off at the door. The cab that would take me to the airport was waiting outside. I picked up my bags, gave my farewell hug and headed to the airport to catch my Etihad flight. Just before the plane ascended above the dust cover of Delhi, I took one long look at the brightly lit city below. It stretched endlessly on all sides.

As the city below slipped by, I put my head back on the seat and closed my eyes, my brain deluged by a million thoughts. A million thoughts about what lay ahead, covered in darkness, waiting to be unveiled by me.

Notes

1. https://www.thehindu.com/business/Rising-suicides-force-AP-ordinance-to-check-microfinance-firms/article15780132.ece
2. Tao Sun, 'The Impact of Global Liquidity on Financial Landscapes and Risks in the ASEAN-5 Countries' (IMF Working Paper No. 15/211, 29 September 2015).
3. According to research firm Tracxn, venture investors poured $229 million into 431 foodtech start-ups in 2015, four times the amount of money and number of businesses as in 2013.
4. Priyanka Pani, 'Housing.com CEO Rahul Yadav Shown the Door', *The Hindu BusinessLine*, 24 January 2018, https://www.thehindubusinessline.com/news/variety/housingcom-ceo-rahul-yadav-shown-the-door/article7374462.ece
5. 'Housing.com's Self-proclaimed "Genius Billionaire Philanthropist" Rahul Yadav Sacked', *DNA*, 1 July 2015, https://www.dnaindia.com/business/report-housingcom-s-self-proclaimed-genius-billionaire-philanthropist-rahul-yadav-sacked-2100694
6. https://yourstory.com/2015/05/powai-valley
7. https://www.youtube.com/watch?v=N9S6XbBuErE

Index